MIGHTY
SPICE
COOKBOOK

MIGHTY
SPICE
COOKBOOK

FAST, FRESH AND VIBRANT DISHES
USING NO MORE THAN 5 SPICES FOR EACH RECIPE

JOHN GREGORY-SMITH

DUNCAN BAIRD PUBLISHERS

LONDON

DEDICATION
To my amazing family who have never stopped supporting me

MIGHTY SPICE
COOKBOOK

JOHN GREGORY-SMITH

Distributed in the USA and Canada by
Sterling Publishing Co., Inc.
387 Park Avenue South
New York, NY 10016-8810

First published in the UK and USA in 2011 by
Duncan Baird Publishers Ltd
Sixth Floor, Castle House
75–76 Wells Street
London W1T 3QH

Managing Editor: Grace Cheetham
Editors: Camilla Davis and Kirty Topiwala
Managing Designer: Manisha Patel
Production: Uzma Taj
Commissioned Photography: William Lingwood
Food Stylist: Aya Nishimura
Prop Stylist: Wei Tang

Library of Congress Cataloging-in-Publication Data available

ISBN: 978-1-84483-996-4

10 9 8 7 6 5 4 3 2 1

Typeset in Myriad Pro and SonKern
Color reproduction by Colourscan, Singapore
Printed in China by Imago

For information about custom editions, special sales, premium and
corporate purchases, please contact Sterling Special Sales Department at
800-805-5489 or specialsales@sterlingpub.com.

PUBLISHER'S NOTE:
While every care has been taken in compiling the recipes for this book,
Duncan Baird Publishers, or any other persons who have been involved
in working on this publication, cannot accept responsibility for any errors
or omissions, inadvertent or not, that may be found in the recipes or text,
nor for any problems that may arise as a result of preparing one of these
recipes. If you are pregnant or breastfeeding or have any special dietary
requirements or medical conditions, it is advisable to consult a medical
professional before following any of the recipes contained in this book.

NOTES ON THE RECIPES:
Unless otherwise stated
• Use large eggs and medium fruit and vegetables
• Use fresh herbs
Measurements
• 1 tsp. = 5ml • 1 tbsp. = 15ml • 1 cup = 240ml

Contents

Introduction

Spices are my favorite things: I love talking about them, cooking with them and eating them. I have always been passionate about them, and have spent the past ten years traveling all over the world to learn everything I can about all the different types. Spices have been used in kitchens for thousands of years, and they are as relevant today as they have always been. They have an amazing history; America was even discovered because of them, but I'll tell you more about that when you're hooked! My book is an introduction to cooking with the spices I love so much, to show you how easy and delicious they are to use.

A few years ago, I quit my job and launched a range of fresh spice pastes—The Mighty Spice Company's Chinese Szechwan, Thai Green Curry and Indian Tandoori spice mixes. Initially these sold exclusively at Selfridges, and then in Harvey Nichols, Fortnum & Mason and a few other stores in London. To say things were challenging is an understatement. I worked seven days a week doing demonstrations, PR, marketing, sales, going to farmers' markets and sorting out millions of things that seemed to go wrong. After two years of meetings, tastings and PowerPoint presentations, I scored every food producer's dream—a contract to supply one of the top UK supermarkets. My products launched on a trial basis at a few select outlets and were soon stocked in 250 stores nationwide. It was a great achievement and I loved doing it, but, due to the recession and a down turn in sales of fresh products, I've taken the decision to put the spice pastes on hold for a while.

While on holiday in Spain with my wonderful cousin Lara, I came up with the idea to write a cookbook on spices. I launched my food brand to get people as excited about cooking spicy food as I was; I wanted to encourage people to get back into their kitchens and cook lovely, interesting and tasty food rather than eat horrid ready-made meals or lazy carryouts. My book had to be an extension of this; something that would get people so excited about cooking that after they read my recipes, they would run to the shop and cook them over and over again, just as Homer did in one episode of The Simpsons: someone offered him something to eat and he ran off to get it before they had a chance to finish their sentence. The guy was then left speaking to a cloud outline of the great man . . . it's a brilliant scene. I spent the next couple of weeks of my holiday drinking rioja, eating tapas and planning my book.

Of course, there are loads of people who like cooking, but not that many who are prepared to give up a normal life to move home, renounce paychecks and then make it work selling spice pastes and developing recipes for a living. My father, in a very old-school English way, sent my mother off to do a Cordon Bleu cooking course before marrying her. God forbid one should not have a decent stuffed chicken breast at home! Amazingly she didn't give him a black eye and they have been happily married ever since. Anyway, she was and is a great cook. As a child my brother, sister and I were never allowed to eat anything processed. No potato chips, candy or store-bought cookies for us.

This might also have had something to do with the fact I was allergic to artificial food additives. Already being an overly hyperactive child, any of these additives sent me into overdrive, literally climbing the walls and banisters a few times. I remember on one occasion buying a very cool Optimus Prime-shaped (this is a Transformer to those not in the know), multicolored gelatin confection. I took my spoils home and showed my mom. She must have got that sinking feeling she did so many times with me as a child, and told me gelatins like that were much nicer cold, so it was best to put it in the refrigerator. Being young and naive I it up. When I returned to claim my treat, a heinous crime had been committed, and it was gone. Who could believe it, in my own home, my own refrigerator?

The fact my mom always gave us fresh homecooked food is definitely how my love of cooking began from a young age. Sadly, it was a bit uncool for a twelve-year-old boy to cook for his friends, so I constantly offered to cook for my amazing family. I have loads of aunts, uncles and cousins, who all have marvelous husbands, wives and a huge flock of kids. I also have my mom and dad, who have always supported me, my brother and his wife, my sister and her husband and my crazy niece and nephew, Daisy and Jake; I love them all very much. Food has always been massively important to my entire family, and I can't think of anything I would rather be doing than cooking up a feast and tucking in with all of them. As a child, being the youngest meant I had to fend for myself and eat fast. I soon realized, however, if I did the cooking the dynamic changed and I could avoid being so low down the pecking order; I was even offered food first, before anyone else.

Both my parents lived abroad when they were little, where they picked up a taste for the exotic; my mother in Pakistan and my father in Turkey. I remember countless curries at my grandparents' house, and became accustomed to fiery chilies and retro curry powders from an early age. I was totally spoiled and taken all over the place by my wonderful parents. Eating always featured, and the second I was old enough I started traveling in search of new and exciting foods. I remember going to Thailand and Hong Kong when I was sixteen, and discovering tom yum goong and dim sum for the first time. There was literally a world of food out there to be discovered and I was keen to get cracking. I loved finding something new and recreating it back at home, and I would go out of my way to find things like fresh curry leaves and the best coconut milk to make the perfect Thai green curry (that's Chaokoh by the way; it just rocks compared to the rest).

I decided to travel around China, Vietnam, Cambodia, Thailand, Malaysia, Singapore, Indonesia, India, Sri Lanka, Morocco, Turkey, Lebanon and Mexico to learn as much as I could about how different countries and cuisines use spices while working on this book. Mothers, aunts, sisters and grannies of the world have these secrets, and it was from those guys I got them. I couldn't wait to get started. I arrived at Heathrow to get my flight to Hong Kong for my first trip, and when I tried to check in the lady told me I was very keen and that check-in was usually only two hours before the flight and that I was a month early! Luckily I managed to change my ticket and made it out. I filled my days in Hong Kong eating dim sum, but it was on my first night that I discovered a wonderful, modern beef dish, which was the inspiration for my Stir-Fried Beef with Black Pepper and Basil (see page 89). It relied on bucket loads of coarsely ground black pepper to give it a flavor and a real kick, balsamic vinegar for seasoning and a massive handful of torn basil. It was exactly my kind of food and I was really excited to see how pepper can be used as the main spice, which is so common in Southeast Asia.

Next I headed to China, which was the most surprising destination food wise. Everyone had said the food in China was, well different, to put it politely. Yes, they eat some mad things, such as scorpion kebabs, sea cucumbers and cats, but they also eat some of the most beautifully cooked, well-balanced food I have ever tasted. Their use of spices, particularly in the Sichuan Province, is phenomenal. I have always loved the tongue-numbing power of the Szechuan peppercorn, so it was fantastic to learn how to use them in harmony with the fiery hot dried chilies of the area, producing full-on flavor without ever masking the other components of the dish.

My trip around China took me to Chengdu, the capital of the Sichuan Province. From here I had arranged to go into the countryside to learn about real Szechuan cooking; real people, cooking with locally grown ingredients to make simple food for their family and friends. Sadly it was not what I expected. My expectation of rolling bamboo-strewn hills turned out to be a high-rise apartment block in downtown Chengdu, and the local villagers a Chengduian family called the Hungs. I still had a great time and learned loads, though. Before cooking we hit a local market and bought fish that were still swimming around in large plastic containers; pork that hung from grim-looking hooks; and a load of fresh fruits and vegetables that put my local supermarket to shame. We returned to their tiny apartment and cooked up a storm. The whole family came over and we ate one of the best meals I have been lucky enough to enjoy. A fiery green peppercorn fish soup, deep-fried pork ribs with Szechuan peppercorns, star anise and chilies and the best rice ever. The ribs were sweet, sour and packed with flavor from the strong spice combination, which regularly features in Sichuan.

The following morning I went to a factory famous for making chilli bean paste, a fermented mix of chillies and soy beans that forms the base of many Sichuan dishes, in Pixan. The paste can be quite difficult to find, so I have made a version which you can make really easily. I use it as the base for my Twice-Cooked Pork (see page 111), but you can also use it for any stir-fry dish.

When we arrived at Pixan I opened the car door to the foulest stench of vinegar, chili and all things wrong my nose had ever smelled. My translator was dry retching and looked deeply disturbed by the whole thing and kept asking if this was what I wanted to do. Sadly it was. We went through rows of huge fermentation tanks covered in filth and loads of sorry-looking staff, with facemasks on or simply bits of cotton wool stuffed up their noses, sorting dry chilies. This was a privately owned chili farm, and all I can say is thank god they would never get through our supermarkets' basic food hygiene tests. It was a shame, but what I love about what I do, is that you have to take the rough with the smooth. Dinner the night before was so smooth and this was so rough!

After traveling all around Southeast Asia I went to India—my favorite country to date—and Sri Lanka. India is amazing; a full-on sensory overload. Everything is good and bad all at once, and nothing makes any sense. You either love it or hate it. I loved every minute I was there. From learning about the heavy use of spices used in Rajasthani cuisine, while everyone threw colored dye at each other celebrating the festival of Holi, to learning about the extremely hot coconut curries of the Syrian Christians in Kerala or getting lost in the luscious, green hills of Munnar.

Markets featured heavily in my travels—I feel very comfortable wandering around them, and one of my favorite markets was Khari Baoli, in Old Delhi. I was taken around this famous spice market by my friend Madhu Gupta. Old Delhi is bonkers; it's like going back in time. Beautiful madness: smelly for the right and wrong reasons, bustling markets alongside abject poverty. It's everything all at once and really, really busy, and I loved it. Open-fronted stores line the streets selling all kinds of spices and cooking ingredients. We pushed through, looking at everything as people shouted, spat, urinated, stared and shopped all around us.

Madhu took me to her favorite masala store, which sold preground masalas in amazing boxes straight from the 1970s. Buying a box of masala should be pretty straightforward, but not in India. What happened next was the most brilliant and bizarre way of buying something. The store had two counters that faced each other and a tiny walkway in between them. You chose what you wanted at counter one and placed your order at counter two, where they gave you a ticket. You then took the ticket back to the original counter to be checked and marked, and then, bear with me, took the same ticket back to the second counter to pay. Finally you took your receipt to counter one to receive your purchase. Are you with me? This is precisely what I love about India; complete organized chaos.

After Delhi, I traveled north to Amritsar in the Punjab. It's the holiest of places for Sikhs, home of the Golden Temple, the Sikhs version of Mecca. The Golden Temple sits in the middle of a huge pool of water, surrounded by a walkway, all within a beautiful, huge, white marble temple complex. People walk in, excitedly take a photo (not just the tourists!) or say a silent prayer and wander around taking it all in. It was peaceful, spiritual and very happy all at once. I know little about religion and less about Sikhism, however, what I do know is they practice tolerance and equality—anyone can enter their amazing temple and eat a free meal at the langer (I'll come to this). If everyone thought in this way a bit more, things would definitely be easier.

Right, moving on to the langer—my reason for traveling to Amritsar (and one of my most remarkable food experiences to date). It's a free kitchen for anyone who needs a meal at the Golden Temple, Sikhs and non-Sikhs alike, and is run by donations and help from volunteers. It's open 24 hours, 365 days a year and serves an average of 40,000 to 60,000 meals a day, consisting of dal, vegetable curry, chapatis and a bright orange dessert. I arrived early in the morning and headed to the kitchen. Everyone sat on the floor podding peas and chopping cauliflowers. They all looked a little baffled as to why I was there, but the peas were arriving by the sack load so there were no complaints. The old guy next to me was a serious podder and raced through them. From an early age I've been oddly competitive, and I must win! Well the competitive John appeared, and before I knew it I was in a silent pea-podding competition. The old guy realized things were hotting up and raised his game. I did well until my useless, untrained pea-podding back gave me trouble. I was flagging; the hands were willing but the back wasn't. A very jolly man offered me a wooden block to sit on; I was back in the game! I whizzed through the peas and thanks to my nonarthritic fingers raced ahead. The old man gave me the look, which was most likely a polite way of saying, "I am here all day, every day; try that for a few years and then we'll chat!"

After a few hours I was offered a tour of the monumental kitchens. We started in the washing section. It was epic, hundreds of people chucking metal plates around, cleaning and drying them as they went along; the noise was deafening. Then we went into the main kitchen where groups of women sat cross-legged rolling chapatis. They rolled one at a time, then hurled them onto a hot plate to cook, chatting the whole time, without breaking into a sweat. As we went farther inside, huge, bath-sized pots of curry cooked fiercely over wooden fires. Sturdy old men lovingly mixed the curries, literally, with rowing oars. I love curry and had a real curry moment here. My guide knew everyone. It was wicked. They all wanted to have photos taken and would insist on seeing them before I went. The tour finished in the dining room where people sat in neat rows on the floor and ate their meal next to whoever they were lucky enough to find. Some went off to carry on with their day and others did a turn in the kitchen to keep the ever-working food machine going. What an incredible thing to do; so generous in a country where so many have so little, and what better expression of generosity than a delicious homecooked meal.

After India, I traveled to the Middle East. It kicked off with a three-day "eatathon" in Istanbul accompanied by my dad. What a city! Split into two sides, European and Asian, with beautiful mosques that dot the skyline, and none more beautiful than the famous Blue Mosque itself. Turkey is the home of the kebab, which is something I am really into. Not those horrid things you eat at 1.00 a.m. after drinking pints of lager, but instead, tender grilled meat, mouth-wateringly spicy salsa, crisp salad, soft flat bread and cool yogurt. We ate like kings and enjoyed everything the city had to offer. I particularly enjoyed the flavor of the wonderful dried Turkish chilies. They have an unique, mild sundried taste, which I discovered when I got home can be substituted with a mix of ordinary dried chili and sun-dried tomatoes.

I also spent a week cooking in Beirut, which is one of the coolest cities I have ever been to. The architecture is a mixture of old Arabic meets slick Parisian, and the people are so very smart and full of optimism. The food was incredible: lots of crisp salads and delicately spiced stews made with loads of garlic and fragrant spices, such as cinnamon and saffron, slowly infused with the meat; a punchy mix of sumac, salt, sesame seeds and dried thyme, called a za'atar blend, generously lathered over grilled or broiled meats and freshly baked flat breads, giving a wonderful sour flavor and bright red color. And I can't forget the national food treasure, kebbe. Kebbe is a mix of finely ground meat, which can be raw or cooked, bulgur wheat, spices, herbs and lemon. My favorite was the raw goat kebbe, which is simply made with young raw goat meat finely ground with salt, bulgur wheat, lemon juice and a huge handful of fresh mint. And what they can't do with an eggplant is not worth knowing—grilled with lemon juice, roasted with spices, mashed with tahini and then cooked with lamb or braised in yogurt. I spent my days cooking, eating and wandering around the city, soaking up the sense of excitement that filled the air.

The last stop on my wondrous journey was Mexico. I had visited Mexico before when I learned little more than how to get a suntan and ask for a beer, "una cerveza por favour." This time around I wanted to avoid the beaches and learn about real Mexican food from real Mexican people. I decided to visit Puebla, Veracruz, Oaxaca and, finally, Mexico City, which, by the way, is one of the great cities of the world. I spent my first week in the capable hands of Jon and Estella, learning about Pueblan cuisine—one of the main cuisines of Mexico and characterized by complex dishes such as the Mole Poblano, which uses chocolate and more than thirty ingredients, including cinnamon, cloves and chilies. They spent hours showing me how to make the perfect sauces. We would always start by dry-roasting spices, tomatillos, onions and garlic in a heavy pan until they were beautifully charred and tender, and then blend them up as the base for the various sauces we made. This gave the sauces a really smoky flavor, which is so typical of Mexican cuisine, and the experience taught me all about the wicked fresh, dried and smoked varieties of chilies that feature so heavily in Mexican cuisine.

Their beautiful home sat on a hillside under the watchful eye of a smoking volcano and a load of mad dogs, and next to the wildest nightly rave in Mexico. Every evening when the sun went down the perfect tranquillity was pierced by a crazy Mexican band, which played the same song repeatedly all night, only stopping to make a very odd squelching noise, a bit like if you trod on a large frog.

As happy as I am trotting around spice-strewn hills, I feel more relaxed strolling around a concrete jungle; after all, London is my home. Mexico City is one of the biggest, if not the biggest, and it was a real treat for me to be there after having gone rural for the best part of three weeks. I based myself in the center, walked everywhere and ate everything. My favorite meal was always breakfast at Café Maque. They made amazing scrambled eggs, which were cooked with really spicy chorizo and chili and served with a rich tomato sauce.

I got back to London and worked up the recipes in this book. I've created them so each one is delicious, interesting and shows how easy it is to cook with spices. Some are versions of traditional recipes, while others take inspiration from different cuisines and cultures. So many of the wonderful people I ate with while traveling brought loads of different dishes to the table for everyone to share. This is a lovely, sociable way to eat, and the recipes in this book have been designed with this in mind.

To keep things really simple, and to help you out on your spice adventure, I have only used up to five spices per recipe, so you will be able to grab everything you need from the local supermarket. There are ten featured spices showcased throughout the book and 25 spices used in the recipes in total. Images of each spice used are pictured with the recipes and a key and description can be found in the spice directory on pages 218–221.

CHAPTER ONE

Soups and Salads

In this chapter you will discover how truly versatile spices can be. They can be used to make something really light and refreshing, warm and smoky and even hot and fiery, and with the right combination you only need to add a few spices to a dish to create an extraordinary result. Fresh peppery ginger and star anise flavor the delicate Chinese Pork Dumpling Soup, for example; a few crushed fennel seeds bring the Pomegranate, Fennel, Orange and Watercress Salad to life; and with only five spices you can make a Singapore Coconut and Shrimp Laksa. This is a dish that traditionally uses loads of different spices, but by balancing the flavors of fragrant lemongrass, hot chili, earthy turmeric, garlic and beautifully sour tamarind you can make this delicious, rich soup without any hassle.

LEFT: Chinese Pork Dumpling Soup (page 15)

Turkish Lentil Soup

SERVES 4
1 cup split red lentils, washed and
    drained
2 tablespoons olive oil
1 teaspoon all-purpose flour
2 teaspoons dried mint
1 teaspoon mild chili powder
1 tablespoon sun-dried tomato paste
    or tomato paste
3¾ cups chicken or vegetable stock
¼ cup bulgur wheat
3½ tablespoons butter (optional)
sea salt and freshly ground black pepper
1 lemon, cut into wedges, to serve

GOES WELL WITH
Moroccan Lemon Chicken
    (page 66)
Persian Saffron and Honey Lamb
    Stew (page 101)
Lebanese Lemon and Vanilla Cake
    (page 192)

1 Put the lentils into a large saucepan over high heat with 3¼ cups water and bring to a boil. Cover, reduce the heat and simmer 15 to 20 minutes until the lentils absorb all the water and are tender. Check them every couple of minutes after the 15-minute mark to make sure they are not burning.

2 Heat the oil in a large saucepan over medium heat and add the flour, mint and chili powder. Stirring continuously, add the sun-dried tomato paste after 10 seconds, then after another 10 seconds tip in 2 tablespoons of the stock to loosen up the mixture. After a couple of seconds, slowly add the rest of the stock, stirring as you go, to make sure there are no lumps. Stir in the cooked lentils and bulgur wheat and season with a really good pinch of salt and pepper. Bring to a boil, then turn down the heat and simmer, stirring occasionally, 10 minutes.

3 Stir in the butter, if using, and serve immediately with wedges of lemon—the juice brings out all the delicious flavors.

Chinese Pork Dumpling Soup

1 To make the dumplings, put all the dumpling ingredients in a large mixing bowl and mix well, using your hands to mash everything together. Make sure all the ingredients are evenly distributed to guarantee maximum flavor. Cover and set aside 30 minutes to let the flavors develop, or overnight in the refrigerator if time allows.

2 Meanwhile, pour the stock into a large saucepan and add the star anise, ginger and garlic. Bring to a boil over high heat, then cover, reduce the heat to low and simmer 10 minutes.

3 Pull off a golf ball-size piece of the pork mixture and roll it into a smooth dumpling using the palms of your hands. Set aside and repeat until all of the pork mixture is used. You should get about 8 dumplings.

4 Using a slotted spoon, carefully drop the dumplings into the saucepan with the spiced stock. Add the scallions, Chinese leaf lettuce, cilantro and soy sauce and gently mix everything together. Bring to a boil, then turn the heat down to low and simmer 8 to 10 minutes until the pork dumplings are cooked through and beautifully tender. You can cut one open to test. Serve immediately so the greens stay lovely and fresh.

SERVES 4

5 cups chicken stock

2 star anise

2-inch piece gingerroot, peeled and roughly sliced

1 garlic clove

4 scallions, cut into thin batons

3 cups shredded Chinese leaf lettuce

1 large handful cilantro leaves, roughly chopped

1 tablespoon soy sauce

FOR THE DUMPLINGS

9 ounces ground pork

1-inch piece gingerroot, peeled and finely grated

2 scallions, finely chopped

1 teaspoon light soy sauce

1 teaspoon sesame oil

GOES WELL WITH

Dongbei Cumin and Cilantro Stir-Fried Lamb (page 99)

Steamed Ginger Custard Pots (page 199)

Singapore Coconut and Shrimp Laksa

SERVES 4

1 teaspoon tamarind paste
1¾ cups coconut milk
9 ounces raw jumbo shrimp, shelled
    and deveined
1¼ cups bean sprouts
4 ounces rice noodles
2 tablespoons vegetable oil
sea salt
cilantro sprigs, to serve

FOR THE SPICE PASTE

2 lemongrass stalks
1 red chili
4 garlic cloves
1 teaspoon shrimp paste
½ teaspoon turmeric
2 tablespoons vegetable oil

GOES WELL WITH

Mango, Orange and Nutmeg
    Cheesecake (page 200)
Vanilla and Honey Syllabub
    (page 202)

1 To prepare the spice paste, remove the really tough outer leaves of the lemongrass and cut off the ends of the stalks. Starting at the fatter end, roughly slice each lemongrass stalk into rings. You should see a purple band in the rings. Stop slicing when there are no more purple bands, as the tops will be too tough to eat. Set the tops aside to add to the laksa later and put the sliced lemongrass in a mini food processor. Add the remaining spice paste ingredients and blend to a smooth paste.

2 Put the tamarind paste and scant ½ cup water in a small bowl. Mix well and leave to stand 5 minutes, or until the paste dissolves, then remove any lumps. Heat a large saucepan over medium heat and spoon in the spice paste. Stir-fry the paste 30 seconds, or until fragrant, then pour in the coconut milk, prepared tamarind and scant 1 cup freshly boiled water and season with a pinch of salt. Mix well, then turn up the heat to high and bring to a boil. Add the shrimp, bean sprouts and lemongrass tops, then turn the heat down to low and simmer, stirring occasionally, 5 minutes, or until the shrimp are pink and are cooked through. Remove the lemongrass tops.

3 Meanwhile, cook the noodles according to the package directions, then drain and drizzle with the oil to prevent sticking. Divide the cooked noodles into four deep bowls and ladle the hot soup over. Add a cilantro sprig to each bowl and serve immediately.

Char-Grilled Halloumi, Tomato and Olive Salad

This is adapted from a salad I had in Istanbul, where they use wonderful Turkish chilies that have a mild, smoky, sun-dried taste. I found that by mixing sun-dried tomatoes and chili flakes you can create a similar flavor.

SERVES 4

9 ounces halloumi, cut into
    ¼-inch-thick slices
⅓ cup pine nuts
9 ounces cherry tomatoes
¾ cup pitted black olives, roughly
    chopped
2 large handfuls basil leaves, roughly
    torn
1 cup sun-dried tomatoes in oil, drained
    and finely chopped
juice of 1 lemon
¼ teaspoon chili flakes
1 tablespoon olive oil, plus extra for
    dressing (optional)
sea salt and freshly ground black pepper

GOES WELL WITH

Marinated Lamb Chops with a Spicy
    Mango Salsa (page 102)
Mexican Cinnamon Peaches
    (page 206)

1 Heat a griddle pan over high heat until smoking, then griddle the halloumi pieces about 30 seconds on each side, or until you can see lovely charred lines. Remove the cheese from the pan and set aside.

2 Heat a small skillet over medium heat. Add the pine nuts and toast 1 to 2 minutes until they are golden brown. They will change color very suddenly, so watch them carefully, and every now and then shake the pan so the nuts move about and don't burn. Transfer the pine nuts to a plate to cool.

3 Cut the cherry tomatoes into different shapes and sizes: lengthwise, crosswise, quarters, and leave some whole. This makes the salad look amazing and more interesting to eat. Put them in a large mixing bowl with the olives, basil, sun-dried tomatoes, lemon juice, chili flakes and half the toasted pine nuts. Season with a small pinch of salt and good pinch of pepper and mix well. There should be enough oil in the sun-dried tomatoes to coat everything. If not, stir in extra olive oil.

4 To serve, heap the cherry tomatoes in a large serving bowl and scatter the remaining pine nuts over. Top the salad with the char-grilled halloumi, then drizzle a tablespoon of olive oil over. Serve immediately with the squeezed lemon halves.

Feta, Walnut and Nigella Seed Salad

1 To make the dressing, whisk the oil and lemon juice in a bowl and season with a good pinch of salt and pepper. Add the scallions and set aside 5 minutes to take the rawness out of the scallions.

2 Put half the chopped walnuts in a large mixing bowl and crumble in half the feta. Pour the dressing over, then chuck in the green chili, tarragon, parsley and mint and toss everything together.

3 Divide the salad onto four serving plates, scatter the nigella seeds and the remaining walnuts and feta cheese over the tops and serve immediately.

SERVES 4
½ cup walnuts, roughly chopped
7 ounces feta
1 green chili, seeded and finely chopped
1 large handful tarragon leaves, roughly chopped
2 large handfuls parsley leaves, roughly chopped
2 large handfuls mint leaves, roughly chopped
1 teaspoon nigella seeds

FOR THE DRESSING
juice of 1 lemon
2 tablespoons olive oil
4 scallions, finely sliced
sea salt and freshly ground black pepper

GOES WELL WITH
Char-Grilled Cilantro and Mint Chicken (page 64)
Creamy Cilantro Swordfish with Red Onion Raita (page 123)
Dark Chocolate, Clove and Cinnamon Brownies (page 196)

Pomegranate, Fennel, Orange and Watercress Salad

This is a great-looking fresh salad, bejeweled with pomegranate seeds and orange segments. It showcases of the lovely fresh aniseed flavor that comes from the finely shaved fennel and lightly crushed fennel seeds, which are used in the dressing and bring everything together.

SERVES 4

1 pomegranate
3 oranges, peeled and cut into segments
½ red chili, seeded and finely chopped
2½ ounces watercress
1 fennel bulb, very thinly sliced or
     shaved with a mandolin

FOR THE DRESSING

1 teaspoon fennel seeds, lightly crushed
juice of 1 lemon
2 tablespoons orange juice
1 tablespoon olive oil
sea salt and freshly ground black pepper

GOES WELL WITH

Broiled Lamb Skewers with a Bulgar
     Wheat Salad (page 106)
Cardamon and Pistachio Nut Kulfi
     (page 205)

1 To make the dressing, whisk all the ingredients together in a mixing bowl, season with a good pinch of salt and pepper and set aside.

2 Roll the pomegranate back and forth a couple of times on a hard surface to loosen the seeds, then cut it in half. Using a wooden spoon, bash the seeds out into a bowl. This can get quite messy, so wear an apron to cover your clothes and put the bowl into the sink while you're bashing—this way any mess can easily be washed away. Remove any white bits from the seeds and drain off the excess juice. Transfer the seeds into a mixing bowl along with the orange segments, red chili, watercress and fennel.

3 Pour the dressing over the salad, toss well and serve immediately.

Chili

I absolutely love chilies—they are my favorite spice. There is something so beautiful and exotic about them; from warming mild chilies to smoky dry chilies or the full-on, punch-in-the-face hot chilies. They are all amazing to cook with.

The chili has a really interesting story. It was discovered when Christopher Columbus bumped into America by accident, while trying to find a faster route to the spice islands of Indonesia. The Europeans weren't very receptive to this odd-tasting spice, but the locals of a certain colony in India, called Goa, went mad for it. It quickly replaced the expensive black pepper as the piquancy in the local Goan food—and eventually made its way into dishes throughout the world.

Fresh chilies are generally red or green, and the smaller they are the hotter they are. You get the wonderful Asian chilies, fat mild jalapeños, fruity hot Caribbean Scotch bonnets and the scorching little bird's-eye chilies that are generally used whole, but, to release even more heat, can be pricked a few times with a sharp knife. When buying chilies, you want to look for ones that are juicy, firm and with a shiny skin. The heat is mainly in the seeds and the thin layer of skin on the inside of the chili, so if you want to avoid the full hit of heat, scrape out the seeds and the thin layer of skin with a teaspoon. Also, a quick rinse will remove even more of the heat. When preparing any sort of chili, please remember not to rub your eyes. Fresh chilies are very robust and will normally last about a week in the refrigerator.

Dry chilies come whole, crushed or powdered and in an array of different strengths. They have a more intense, full-bodied, smoky flavor than fresh chilies, and the powders also provide a beautiful red color. Most of the dried and powdered chilies available will last about six months in a dry, airtight container if it is kept out of direct sunlight.

If you get a bit overexcited and chuck too much chili into your wonderful culinary creations, coconut milk, cream or plain yogurt will help take some of the heat out. And if you have a mouthful of something that's a bit too adventurous, don't grab for the water—this will only make the hot sensation worse. Instead, have some yogurt, milk or plain rice to take away the intensely spicy edge!

Chinese Tiger Salad

This crunchy salad is one of my favorite side dishes. In China, it is served as an appetizer to snack on with a drink or to go with kebabs. It's also the perfect accompaniment to a piping hot stir-fry and rice. I always make enough to roll up in tortilla wraps with chicken for lunch the next day.

SERVES 4

6 scallions, finely sliced on a diagonal
1 red bell pepper, seeded and thinly sliced
1 green bell pepper, seeded and thinly sliced
2 baby leeks, halved lengthwise and thinly sliced
2 large handfuls cilantro leaves, finely chopped
1 red chili, thinly sliced
sesame seeds, to serve

FOR THE DRESSING

2 tablespoons soy sauce
1 tablespoon rice wine vinegar
1 teaspoon sesame oil
1 tablespoon sesame seeds
½ teaspoon chili flakes

GOES WELL WITH

Stir-Fried Beef with Black Pepper and Basil (page 89)
Guyi Cumin, Chili and Soy Ribs (page 112)

1   Whisk the dressing ingredients together in a large bowl.
2   Add the scallions, red and green peppers, baby leeks, cilantro and red chili, then mix everything together until well combined. Scatter sesame seeds over and serve.

Coconut and Chili Kerabu Salad

1. To make the dressing, whisk the fish sauce, lime juice and sugar together in a large bowl. Grate the gingerroot into the bowl, discarding the fibrous bits, and mix well.
2. Scatter the onion over the dressing and mix well, then set aside 5 to 10 minutes. This takes the rawness out of the onion.
3. Meanwhile, toast the coconut in a small skillet over medium heat, stirring continuously, 30 to 40 seconds until the coconut turns a lovely golden brown. Tip it onto a plate and set aside.
4. To assemble the salad, add the red pepper, bean sprouts, red chili and mint to the onion mixture and toss until all the ingredients are well coated. Transfer to a serving bowl, scatter the roasted coconut over the top and serve immediately.

SERVES 4

½ red onion, thinly sliced
2 tablespoons shredded coconut
1 red bell pepper, seeded and thinly sliced
2¼ cups bean sprouts
½ red chili, seeded and finely chopped
1 small handful mint leaves, roughly chopped

FOR THE DRESSING

4 tablespoons fish sauce
juice of 2 limes
2 teaspoons sugar
1-inch piece gingerroot, peeled

GOES WELL WITH

Za'atar Lamb Cutlets (page 104)
Char Kueh Toew (Fried Rice Noodles with Shrimp and Egg) (page 193)
Lemongrass and Ginger Rum Cocktail (page 216)

Jetalah Pineapple, Cucumber and Chili Salad

This delicious Malay salad will bring a little sunshine to your table. Naz, a fantastic chef and friend of mine, taught me how to make this salad when we cooked a meal together in the most beautiful spice garden in Penang. We ate our dinner sitting on a terrace overlooking the ocean, with the sun going down and the air thick with the smell of cardamom, cloves and cinnamon.

SERVES 4

½ red onion, thinly sliced
6 tablespoons rice wine or apple cider vinegar
2 teaspoons sugar
½ pineapple, peeled
½ cucumber, halved lengthwise
1 large tomato, seeded and roughly chopped
1 red chili, seeded and finely sliced
1 tablespoon freshly ground black pepper
sea salt

GOES WELL WITH

Coconut and Lemongrass Salmon Curry (page 135)
Sri Lankan Fried Potatoes (page 166)
Lebanese Lemon and Vanilla Cake (page 198)

1 Put the onion, vinegar and sugar in a large mixing bowl. Season with a pinch of salt, mix well and set aside 5 to 10 minutes. This takes the rawness out of the onion.

2 Cut the pineapple into quarters, then remove and discard the hard central core from each piece and cut the flesh into thin slices. Next, run a teaspoon down the middle of the 2 halves of cucumber, removing the seeds as you go. Slice the flesh into thin half-moon pieces.

3 Put the pineapple, cucumber, tomato, red chili and black pepper into the bowl with the onion mixture, toss everything together until well combined, and serve immediately.

Fattoush Salad

This is one of those perfect dishes. It is full of sweet and juicy vegetables that are complemented with a tangy dressing made with both lemon and sumac. It looks fantastic and, with all the different textures, it is interesting to eat, too. It is extremely refreshing on a hot day, and on cold days it brings the sunshine straight to you. While delicious eaten on its own, it is also great with any grilled or broiled meat, char-grilled halloumi or a fragrant stew.

1 Toast the pita bread until golden and set aside to cool.
2 Whisk together the dressing ingredients in a large mixing bowl and season with a good pinch of salt and pepper. Add the cucumber, onion, olives, cherry tomatoes, mint and parsley and toss everything together.
3 Once the pita bread is cool, crunch half of it between your hands and sprinkle the pieces over the salad. Toss everything together until well combined.
4 Transfer the salad to a large serving bowl, then break the rest of the pita over the top and serve immediately.

SERVES 4
2 pita breads
1 cucumber, seeded and roughly chopped
½ small red onion, thinly sliced
1 cup pitted black olives
1½ cups halved small cherry tomatoes
1 large handful mint leaves, roughly chopped
1 large handful parsley leaves, roughly chopped

FOR THE DRESSING
3 tablespoons olive oil
juice of 1 lemon
¼ teaspoon sumac
sea salt and freshly ground black pepper

GOES WELL WITH
Roast Lebanese Leg of Lamb with Spiced Lentil Puree (page 97)
Falafel Burgers with a Yogurt and Tahini Dip (page 150)

Kandy Black Pepper and Soy Eggplant Salad

SERVES 4

4 tablespoons vegetable oil
1 eggplant, cut into ⅝-inch-thick
    wedges
1 garlic clove
1 tablespoon tomato paste
2 tablespoons soy sauce
a pinch of sugar
1 teaspoon freshly ground black pepper
juice of ½ lime
½ red onion, finely chopped
½ cup quartered cherry tomatoes
1 green bell pepper, seeded and finely
    chopped
½ red chili, seeded and finely chopped

GOES WELL WITH
Pueblan Almond Duck (page 82)
Steamed Cod in a Banana Leaf
    (page 126)

1 Heat the oil in a large skillet over medium heat and add the eggplant wedges, stirring well to make sure all the pieces are coated in the oil. Cook, stirring occasionally, 6 minutes, then add the garlic. Continue to cook 2 minutes, or until the eggplant is tender and cooked through and the garlic is just turning golden. Stir in the tomato paste, soy sauce, sugar, pepper and lime juice and cook 1 minute longer.

2 Transfer to a large mixing bowl and add the onion, cherry tomatoes, green pepper and red chili. Toss together and serve immediately.

Asparagus, Green Bean and Wasabi Salad

I love the simple, clean flavors of this salad—the crisp beans, tart dressing and the layers of spice from the fresh chili and the nose-tingling wasabi. If you eat with your eyes, the deep red flecks of chili against the bright green beans will draw you into their world as well.

SERVES 4
4 ounces asparagus, hard ends of stalks
    snapped off and roughly chopped
2 cups halved thin green beans
2/3 cup shelled edamame beans
sea salt

FOR THE DRESSING
juice of 1 lemon
1 tablespoon olive oil
¾ teaspoon wasabi paste
½ red chili, seeded and finely chopped

GOES WELL WITH
Vietnamese Chicken with Chili and
    Lemongrass (page 56)
Stir-Fried Beef with Black Pepper
    and Basil (page 89)

1 Add a pinch of salt to a large saucepan of water and bring to a boil. Add the asparagus and cook 2 minutes, then add the green beans and cook 2 minutes longer. Add the edamame beans and continue cooking 2 minutes, then drain the vegetables and rinse them under cold water until they are completely cool. Shake off as much water as possible.

2 Whisk the dressing ingredients together in a large mixing bowl and season with a good pinch of salt. Add the cooked beans, toss so they are well covered in dressing and serve immediately.

Szechuan Chicken and Cucumber Salad

This is a brilliantly hot and fresh Chinese salad—the spicy chicken and cooling cucumber balance each other perfectly. You can cook the chicken any way you like—roast, boil, fry—whichever you find easiest. The Chinese believe eating the skin of the chicken is good for your skin, so if you're feeling in need of some rejuvenation leave it on (although I prefer it without.)

1 To make the dressing, heat the oil in a small saucepan over low heat 2 minutes, or until a few tiny bubbles start to appear. Remove the pan from the heat and add the chili flakes, Szechuan pepper, sugar, soy sauce and lemon juice. Whisk everything together and set aside 5 to 10 minutes. This lets all those lovely flavors infuse with the oil.

2 Meanwhile, cut the chicken into bite-size pieces. Cut the cucumber in half lengthwise and scrape out the seeds with a teaspoon, then slice the flesh into thin half-moon chunks.

3 Put the chicken, cucumber and cilantro into a mixing bowl and pour the dressing over. Toss everything together until well combined and serve immediately.

SERVES 4
2½ cups cooked chicken with all the skin and bones removed
1 cucumber
1 handful cilantro leaves, roughly chopped

FOR THE DRESSING
3 tablespoons vegetable oil
2 tablespoons mild chili flakes
1 teaspoon ground Szechuan pepper
½ teaspoon sugar
2 tablespoons light soy sauce
juice of ½ lemon

GOES WELL WITH
Sticky Szechuan Pork with Sesame Seeds (page 108)
Beijing Teahouse Vegetable Stir-Fry (page 169)
Cambodian Caramelized Ginger Bananas with Vanilla Ice Cream (page 212)

Indian Chicken, Pomegranate and Herb Salad

SERVES 4

1 pound 2 ounces skinless, boneless
    chicken breasts, cut into
    bite-size pieces
2 tablespoons olive oil
1 pomegranate
2 large handfuls mint leaves, roughly
    chopped
2 large handfuls cilantro leaves, roughly
    chopped
3 large carrots, peeled and grated
juice of 1 lemon

FOR THE SPICE PASTE

2 tablespoons olive oil
½ teaspoon turmeric
½ teaspoon mild chili powder
1 teaspoon garam masala
2 garlic cloves
1 teaspoon sea salt

GOES WELL WITH

Herb and Spice Pilaf Rice (page 181)
Sri Lankan Fried Rice with Cashew
    Nuts and Egg (page 182)

1 To make the spice paste, put all the ingredients in a mini food processor and grind to a smooth paste. Scrape the paste into a mixing bowl, add the chicken and mix well, making sure the chicken is completely coated. Cover and leave 30 minutes, or overnight if time allows.

2 Heat the oil in a skillet over medium heat. Add the chicken and cook 5 to 6 minutes on each side until golden, crisp and cooked through.

3 Roll the pomegranate back and forth a couple of times on a hard surface to loosen the seeds, then cut it in half. Using a wooden spoon, bash the seeds out into a bowl. This can get quite messy, so wear an apron to cover your clothes and put the bowl into the sink while you're bashing—this way any mess can easily be washed away. Remove any white bits from the seeds and drain off the excess juice.

4 Transfer the pomegranate seeds to a serving bowl along with the mint, cilantro, carrots and lemon juice and mix well. Scatter the cooked chicken pieces and any juices over the top and serve immediately.

Char-Grilled Moroccan Chicken, Sprouting Broccoli and Couscous Salad

1 Heat a skillet over medium heat. Add the almonds and gently toast, shaking the pan occasionally, 4 to 6 minutes until the almonds are a beautiful golden brown. Transfer the nuts to a plate to cool.

2 To make the spice paste, put all the ingredients in a mini food processor and blend to a smooth paste. Transfer to a large mixing bowl.

3 Add the chicken to the spice paste and mix well, making the sure the chicken thighs are completed coated. Cover and leave to marinate 30 minutes, or overnight in the refrigerator if time allows.

4 Heat a griddle pan over high heat and griddle the chicken 5 to 6 minutes on each side, or until golden and cooked through with the lovely char marks form. Set aside for a few minutes to rest, then slice into thin strips.

5 Tip the couscous into a large mixing bowl and pour 1 cup warm water over. Cover with plastic wrap and leave to stand 10 minutes, or until tender, then fluff with a fork to separate the grains.

6 Meanwhile, bring a saucepan of water to a boil. Add the broccoli and cook 3 to 4 minutes until just tender. Drain in a colander, then refresh in cold water and drain again.

7 Put the prepared chicken, broccoli, almonds, mint, lemon juice and oil into the mixing bowl with the couscous and season with a good pinch of salt and pepper. Toss everything together until well combined and serve immediately.

SERVES 4
⅓ cup almonds
1 pound 2 ounces boneless, skinless chicken thighs
¾ cup couscous
1½ cups roughtly chopped sprouting broccoli
2 large handfuls mint leaves, roughly chopped
juice of 1 lemon
2 tablespoons olive oil
sea salt and freshly ground black pepper

FOR THE SPICE PASTE
1 garlic clove
1 red chili, seeded
1-inch piece gingerroot, peeled and roughly chopped
1 large handful mint leaves, roughly chopped
1 teaspoon ground cumin
½ teaspoon turmeric
juice of 1 lemon
2 tablespoons olive oil
½ teaspoon sea salt

GOES WELL WITH
Tropical Fruit Salad with a Chili, Star Anise, Cinnamon and Lime Dressing (page 210)

Guacamole and Shrimp Salad

SERVES 4

2 ripe avocados, peeled and pitted
juice of 3 limes
2 tablespoons plain yogurt (optional)
4 scallions, finely chopped
1 red chili, seeded and finely chopped
2 large handfuls cilantro leaves, roughly
    chopped
9 ounces cooked and shelled jumbo
    shrimp
¼ cucumber, seeded and finely chopped
sea salt and freshly ground black pepper
smoked paprika, to serve
tortilla chips, to serve

GOES WELL WITH

Tamarind and Lemongrass Chicken
    Stir-Fry (page 59)
Stir-Fried Squid with Chili and
    Cilantro (page 145)
Mango, Orange and Nutmeg
    Cheesecake (page 201)

1 Put the avocados and lime juice in a large mixing bowl and mash together with
   a fork until it resemble a chunky paste. If your avocados aren't very creamy in texture,
   stir the yogurt into the mixture.

2 Chuck in the scallions, red chili and cilantro and season with a good pinch of salt and
   pepper. Mix everything together well, then press plastic wrap on the surface and
   refrigerate until you're ready to eat.

3 When you're ready to serve, add the shrimp and cucumber to the avocado mixture
   and very gently mix it all together. Sprinkle some paprika over, then serve either
   chilled or at room temperature with lots of tortilla chips for dipping.

Broiled Haddock, Apple and Cilantro Salad with a Lemongrass Dressing

1 Pour the lemon juice over the apple slices to stop them discoloring and set aside.

2 To prepare the dressing, remove the really tough outer leaves from the lemongrass and cut off the ends of the stalks. Starting at the fatter end, roughly slice each lemongrass stalk into rings. You should see a purple band in the rings. Stop slicing when there are no more purple bands and discard the rest of the lemongrass, as it will be too tough to eat. Give the lemongrass slices a quick blast in a mini food processor until they are very finely chopped, then chuck into a mixing bowl with the other dressing ingredients, whisk together and set aside.

3 Meanwhile, preheat the broiler to high. Brush the fish with a little oil and place under the hot broiler 3 to 4 minutes on each sideuntil the fish is opaque and flaky, then cut into bite-size pieces.

4 Put the cilantro leaves and stalks into a large serving bowl with the mint, onion, apples and three-quarters of the dressing and toss together. Scatter the fish pieces over the top, spoon the remaining dressing over the fish and serve immediately.

SERVES 4

juice of ½ lemon

4 green apples, peeled, cored and sliced

4 haddock fillets, about 7 ounces each, skinned

olive oil, for brushing

4 large handfuls cilantro sprigs, leaves roughly chopped and stalks finely chopped

4 large handfuls mint leaves, roughly chopped

2 red onions, thinly sliced

FOR THE DRESSING

4 lemongrass stalks

2 tablespoons fish sauce

2 teaspoons sugar

juice of 2 limes

½ teaspoon mild chili powder

GOES WELL WITH

Moroccan Lemon Chicken (page 67)

Tomato and Coconut Rice (page 187)

Squid and Chorizo Salad

This is such an vibrantly colored salad, packed full of different textures and flavors that excite the palette. The fresh chili, olives, red onion and parsley create a eastern Mediterranean base, but it's the chorizo that's the real star. It adds crispiness, which works well with the soft squid, and offers loads of flavor from all the paprika and spices that ooze when it's cooked. The fresh lime juice then brings the whole salad together.

1 Slice the squid into rings, keeping the tentacles whole.
2 Heat the oil in a large skillet over medium heat, then add the chorizo and cook 3 to 4 minutes, stirring occasionally, until the chorizo starts to color and crisp. Scatter the squid into the same pan and stir thoroughly. Cook 2 to 3 minutes until the squid is pale and cooked through. Remove the pan from the heat, add the lime juice and set aside until you are ready to eat.
3 To assemble the salad, put the squid, chorizo and their juices into a serving bowl. Add the olives, onion, parsley and red chili and season with a good pinch of salt and pepper. Toss everything together so the lovely spicy red chorizo and fresh lime juices coat all the other ingredients and serve immediately.

SERVES 4
12 ounces baby squid, dressed
2 tablespoons olive oil
3 ounces chorizo, roughly chopped
juice of 1 lime
1 cup pitted black olives, roughly chopped
1 red onion, finely chopped
2 large handfuls parsley leaves, roughly chopped
1 red chili, seeded and cut into thin strips
sea salt and fresh ground black pepper

GOES WELL WITH
Estella's Mexican Beef-Filled Peppers with a Pecan Sauce (page 92)
Mexican Cinnamon Peaches (page 206)
Chili Passionfruit Martinis (page 214)

Shrimp and Lemongrass Rice Noodle Salad

SERVES 4

9 ounces thin rice noodles
2 tablespoons vegetable oil
9 ounces cooked and shelled jumbo
   shrimp
1 red bell pepper, seeded and finely
   chopped
2 large handfuls cilantro leaves, finely
   chopped

FOR THE DRESSING

3 lemongrass stalks
juice of 1 lime
¼ teaspoon sugar
½ red chili, seeded and finely chopped
2 tablespoons soy sauce
2 tablespoons vegetable oil
¼ teaspoon freshly ground black pepper
½ tablespoon sesame oil
1 teaspoon sea salt

GOES WELL WITH

Fried Steaks with Black Pepper Dip
   (page 88)
Stir-Fried Squid with Chili and
   Cilantro (page 145)

1 Cook the noodles according to the package directions, then drain in a colander and rinse with cold water. Once the noodles are cold, squeeze out any excess water with your hands, so they are really dry. Rice noodles are very sturdy and won't break, so give them a good squeeze, otherwise you'll end up with a watery salad.

2 Drizzle the oil over the prepared noodles and mix well. This stops them from sticking. Use a knife to cut the noodles in half and then in half again to help them to mix better with the other salad ingredients.

3 To prepare the dressing, remove the really tough outer leaves from the lemongrass and cut off the ends of the stalks. Starting at the fatter end, roughly slice each lemongrass stalk into rings. You should see a purple band in the rings. Stop slicing when there are no more purple bands and discard the rest of the lemongrass, as it will be too tough to eat. Give the lemongrass slices a quick blast in a mini food processor until they are very finely chopped, then chuck into a large mixing bowl with the other dressing ingredients and whisk together.

4 Add the noodles, shrimp, red pepper and cilantro to the dressing and mix well. Either serve immediately or chill in the refrigerator to let the flavors really develop.

Vietnamese Shrimp, Cucumber and Mint Salad

1 Heat a skillet over medium heat. Add the peanuts and gently toast, shaking the pan occasionally, 2 to 3 minutes until the peanuts are a beautiful golden brown. Transfer the nuts to a plate to cool.

2 To prepare the dressing, remove the really tough outer leaves of the lemongrass and cut off the ends of the stalks. Starting at the fatter end, roughly slice each lemongrass stalk into rings. You should see a purple band in the rings. Stop slicing when there are no more purple bands and discard the rest of the lemongrass, as it will be too tough to eat. Give the lemongrass slices a quick blast in a mini food processor until they are very finely chopped. Transfer to a large mixing bowl and whisk together with the other dressing ingredients.

3 Put the shrimp, cucumber, carrot, scallions, red chili, mint and peanuts into a large serving bowl. Pour the dressing over, toss everything together until well combined and serve immediately.

SERVES 4
⅓ cup unsalted peanuts
9 ounces cooked and shelled jumbo shrimp
½ cucumber, peeled and sliced
1 large carrot, peeled and thinly sliced
2 scallions, finely chopped
½ red chili, seeded and finely chopped
1 large handful mint leaves, roughly chopped

FOR THE DRESSING
2 lemongrass stalks
juice of 1 lime
1 tablespoon fish sauce
1 teaspoon sugar

GOES WELL WITH
Tamarind and Lemongrass Chicken Stir-Fry (page 59)
Cha Ca La Vong (Vietnamese Turmeric- and Chili-Spiced Cod with Rice Noodles, Peanuts and Herbs) (page 118)

Lemongrass

Lemongrass, as its name suggests, has a delicious, earthy lemony flavor, and is native to India and Sri Lanka. This citrusy spice goes hand in hand with coconut milk, and is used to flavor all sorts of curries, soups, stir-frys, marinades and even teas and desserts all over Asia. The strongly scented oil is used as a mosquito repellent and a natural preservative, which is so effective it is even put on ancient papyrus manuscripts to help preserve them for generations to come.

A perennial grass, lemongrass grows in thick clumps with a fat stalk and a tall wispy top. All the flavor is in the stalk, so you want to look for lovely fat, pale-colored stalks of lemongrass and avoid anything that looks tired and shriveled. Fresh lemongrass keeps its flavor for a couple of weeks in the refrigerator.

You can buy lemongrass fresh, dried (which needs to be soaked for a few hours before being used) powdered and in brine (which is very soft so you can just chop it up as desired.) I have to say, for me, however, the point of lemongrass is the wonderful fresh flavor it gives, and I think only the fresh version delivers this.

Lemongrass is a tough spice that you need to prepare properly so you don't get any woody shards in your delicious meal. The first way to prepare your lemongrass is to simply bash the fat end of the stalks with a spoon, add the stalks to whatever you're making and then fish them out before serving. This way you get all the flavor and none of the texture. The second way is to remove the really tough outer leaves and cut off the tip at the fat end. Then, starting at the fat end, thinly slice the lemongrass into rings. You will see a purple band in the rings as you slice; once these stop discard the rest, as it will be too tough to eat. Finely chop the sliced rings or, alternatively, use a mini food processor to finely chop them. This method is perfect for stir-frys, curry pastes and salad dressings.

Broiled Monkfish Salad with a Roasted Red Pepper, Garlic and Chili Dressing

SERVES 4

12 ounces monkfish fillets, skinned and boned
2½ ounces arugula
1 small handful parsley leaves, finely chopped

FOR THE DRESSING

2 red chilies
2 red bell peppers, quartered and seeded
2 garlic cloves, unpeeled
1 tablespoon olive oil, plus extra for brushing
scant ½ cup plain yogurt
¼ teaspoon smoked paprika
juice of 1 lemon
sea salt and freshly ground black pepper

GOES WELL WITH

Fried Steaks with Black Pepper Dip (page 88)
Nasi Goreng (Indonesian Fried Rice) (page 186)

1 Preheat the oven to 400°F. To make the dressing, prick the red chilies with a sharp knife to stop them exploding in the oven, then put them in a roasting tray with the red peppers and garlic. Drizzle the oil over, season with a good pinch of salt and pepper and mix well with your hands. Roast 20 to 25 minutes until everything is golden and the peppers are beautifully soft and sweet. Set aside to cool.

2 To make the dressing, finely chop half the peppers and put them in a mixing bowl. Roughly chop the other half into bite-size pieces and set aside. Cut off the tops from the chilies and carefully peel away their skins. Slice them open and scrape out and discard the seeds, then put the chili flesh in a mini food processor. Squeeze the garlic cloves out of their skins and add to the processor. Season with a pinch of salt and pepper and grind to a smooth paste. Transfer to the mixing bowl with the finely chopped peppers, then tip in the yogurt, paprika and lemon juice. Mix well and set aside.

3 Meanwhile, preheat the broiler to high. Brush the monkfish with a little oil and place under the hot broiler 3 to 4 minutes on each side, or until the flesh is milky white and firm to the touch. Thinly slice the monkfish and carefully toss it in the dressing.

4 To serve, toss the arugula, parsley and remaining peppers together and divide onto four plates. Spoon the tender, creamy monkfish on top and serve immediately with any remaining dressing dolloped over.

CHAPTER TWO

Poultry

I guarantee this chapter will get you excited about chicken and duck! Here you'll find stir-frys, stews, broiled chicken and five different curries—all of which are made with five or fewer spices. Dive into the recipes and savor the tastes. I love how the flavor of Szechuan peppercorns and dried chilies, when added to the hot oil at the start of the stir-frying, for example, permeates the entire Gung Bao Chicken with their fragrant heat. (I picked this tip up in China and now follow this step whenever I make a Chinese stir-fry.) Less can always be more when using spices, and the Char-Grilled Cilantro and Mint Chicken demonstrates this concept perfectly. By adding just a little garam masala to a herby marinade, the dish gains a real depth of flavor. It couldn't get any simpler than that!

LEFT: Gung Bao Chicken (page 60)

Coconut and Ginger Chicken Stir-Fry

This is a South Indian take on a stir-fry with just a tiny bit of sauce to coat the chicken. It's perfect with dal and rice—they're best friends. I like this dish very hot and ususally use double the amount of chili powder. Make it with the normal amount to begin with and see what you think—you can always add more at the end, but taking it out would be a real task.

SERVES 4

1 pound 2 ounces boneless, skinless chicken breasts, cut into ¾-inch cubes
2 teaspoons garam masala
1 teaspoon chili powder
1 teaspoon sea salt
2 tablespoons vegetable oil
a large pinch dried curry leaves, plus extra to serve
1 red onion, finely chopped
1-inch piece gingerroot, peeled and finely chopped
1 tablespoon white wine vinegar
scant 1 cup coconut milk
steamed rice or dal, to serve

GOES WELL WITH

Chili and Basil Scallops (page 146)
Char Kueh Toew (Fried Rice Noodles with Shrimp and Egg) (page 193)

1 Put the chicken, garam masala, chili powder and salt in a large bowl and mix until all the chicken is well coated. Cover and set aside 30 minutes, or leave overnight in the refrigerator if time allows.

2 Heat a wok over medium heat and add the oil. When the oil is hot, add the curry leaves, onion and ginger to the wok and stir-fry 3 to 4 minutes until the onion is just turning golden. Turn the heat up to high, add the chicken and stir-fry 3 to 4 minutes longer until the chicken is starting to turn golden brown.

3 Pour in the white wine vinegar and coconut milk and cook 1 to 2 minutes until the sauce reduces to coat the chicken in a thin layer and the chicken is cooked through and tender.

4 Finally, rub extra dried curry leaves between your hands so they break up and scatter them over the chicken. Mix well and serve immediately with rice or dal.

Vietnamese Chicken with Chili and Lemongrass

SERVES 4

6 lemongrass stalks, plus extra stalks
   to serve
2 tablespoons vegetable oil
4 garlic cloves, finely chopped
1 red chili, seeded and finely chopped
1 pound 2 ounces boneless, skinless
   chicken thighs, cut into bite-size
   pieces
2 tablespoons fish sauce
1 tablespoon soy sauce
a pinch of sugar
1 handful cilantro leaves, roughly
   chopped
rice noodles, to serve

GOES WELL WITH

Kandy Black Pepper and Soy
   Eggplant Salad (page 34)
Surf and Turf Noodles (page 192)

1 To prepare the lemongrass, remove the really tough outer leaves and cut off the
ends of the stalks. Starting at the fatter end, roughly slice each lemongrass stalk into
rings. You should see a purple band in the rings. Stop slicing when there are no more
purple bands and discard the rest of the lemongrass, as it will be too tough to eat.
Give the lemongrass slices a quick blast in a mini food processor until they are very
finely chopped.

2 Heat a wok over high heat and add the oil. Once the oil is smoking, chuck in the
lemongrass, garlic and red chili and stir-fry 10 seconds, or until fragrant. Add
the chicken and stir-fry 3—4 minutes longer until the chicken is golden and
cooked through.

3 Tip in the fish sauce, soy sauce and sugar and stir-fry 30 seconds longer, then chuck
in the cilantro. Serve immediately with rice noodles and the extra lemongrass stalks.

Tamarind and Lemongrass Chicken Stir-Fry

This simple stir-fry relies on lemongrass, garlic and chili flakes to give it a real punch, while the ground coriander provides the perfect background warmth. Like every great dish, it needs seasoning. The salt element comes from the stringent fish sauce and the sourness from the beautiful tamarind water, which also works to bring all the flavors together perfectly.

1 To prepare the lemongrass, remove the really tough outer leaves and cut off the ends off the stalks. Starting at the fatter end, roughly slice each lemongrass stalk into rings. You should see a purple band in the rings. Stop slicing when there are no more purple bands and discard the rest of the lemongrass, as it will be too tough to eat. Put the lemongrass slices in a mini food processor with the garlic and grind to a smooth paste.

2 Transfer the paste to a large mixing bowl and add the chicken, chili flakes, coriander, sugar and fish sauce. Mix until all of the chicken is well coated, then cover and leave to marinate 30 minutes, or overnight in the refrigerator if time allows.

3 Put the tamarind paste and a scant ½ cup water in a small bowl and mix well. Leave to stand 5 minutes, or until the paste dissolves, then remove any lumps.

4 Heat the oil in a large wok over high heat. Once smoking, add the marinated chicken and the red pepper and stir-fry 3 to 4 minutes until the chicken is starting to turn golden brown. Pour in the tamarind water and soy sauce and stir-fry 3 to 4 minutes longer until the chicken is cooked through and tender and the sauce reduces right down and is beautifully sticky. Serve immediately.

SERVES 4
2 lemongrass stalks
3 garlic cloves
1 pound 2 ounces boneless, skinless chicken thighs, cut into bite-size pieces
1 teaspoon chili flakes
2 teaspoons ground coriander
1 teaspoon sugar
1½ tablespoons fish sauce
1 teaspoon tamarind paste
2 tablespoons vegetable oil
1 red bell pepper, seeded and cut into bite-size pieces
1 tablespoon soy sauce

GOES WELL WITH
Alleppy Shrimp Curry (page 136)
Nasi Goreng (Indonesian Fried Rice) (page 186)

Gung Bao Chicken

I learned how to make this classic Chinese dish in Beijing. On a snowy winter's morning I took a cab to a *houtong* (traditional Chinese house) in the north of the city to do some cooking. The taxi driver dropped me off and I walked along the narrow streets, shivering, looking for the right house, which turned out to be a few tiny rooms around a courtyard. So in a freezing kitchen, my host, the cooking teacher Cheng Yi, and I made a superb lunch, including this fiery, warming chicken. A good meal in China is always followed by tea, so after we'd eaten we sipped on a lovely hot brew and watched the snow fall thickly in the stone courtyard outside, like a scene from the film *Crouching Tiger, Hidden Dragon*.

SERVES 4

⅓ cup unsalted peanuts
1 pound 2 ounces boneless, skinless chicken breasts, cut into ¾-inch cubes
1 tablespoon cornstarch
4 tablespoons light soy sauce
2 tablespoons vegetable oil
1 teaspoon Szechuan peppercorns
2 dried red chilies, roughly chopped
2 garlic cloves, thinly sliced
1-inch piece gingerroot, peeled and thinly sliced
4 scallions, roughly chopped

GOES WELL WITH

Chinese Pork Dumpling Soup (page 15)
Crispy Szechuan Tofu (page 167)

1 Heat a skillet over medium heat. Add the peanuts and gently toast, shaking the pan occasionally, 2 to 3 minutes until the peanuts are a beautiful golden brown. Transfer the nuts to a plate to cool.

2 Put the chicken, cornstarch and half the soy sauce in a large mixing bowl and mix until all of the chicken is well coated. Cover and set aside 10 minutes.

3 Heat a wok over medium heat and add the oil. Once the oil is hot, remove the wok from the heat and throw in the Szechuan peppercorns and dried red chilies. Stir continuously 20 to 30 seconds until the chilies starts to turn light brown in color.

4 Reheat the wok over high heat, then add the chicken. Fry 2 to 3 minutes until just starting to turn golden, then add the garlic, ginger, scallions and peanuts. Stir-fry 1 to 2 minutes longer until the chicken is cooked through and tender.

5 Pour the remaining soy sauce over, mix everything together and serve immediately.

Vietnamese Star Anise and Lemongrass Chicken Claypot

I first tried this at the popular Highway 4 Restaurant in Hanoi with my brother. Sitting at the bar waiting to meet the owner of the restaurant, my brother told me about an old school friend, Dan, who had moved to Vietnam and he hadn't seen for eighteen years. At that moment, in one of the strangest coincidences, in walked the restaurant owner—Dan. It was amazing, two old mates reunited Facebook-free in downtown Hanoi. He treated us to an epic meal that included this wonderful claypot dish.

1 Bash the fat ends of the lemongrass stalks a couple of times with a heavy spoon to help release their delicious flavor.

2 Heat the oil in a large saucepan over medium heat, then throw in the star anise. Cook about 10 seconds until fragrant, then add the onion and stir-fry 5 to 6 minutes until soft. Throw in the garlic, mix well and cook, stirring occasionally, 1 minute.

3 Add the chicken, lemongrass, red chili, fish sauce, sugar, lime juice and the chicken stock, which should just cover everything. Give the ingredients a really good stir and then bring to a boil. Cover, reduce the heat to low and simmer 20 minutes, or until the chicken is cooked through and tender. Remove the lid, increase the heat to medium and cook 5 minutes to reduce the liquid slightly. The final sauce should still be fairly thin.

4 Remove the lemongrass and star anise and serve immediately with rice.

SERVES 4

3 lemongrass stalks
1 tablespoon vegetable oil
1 star anise
1 onion, finely sliced
2 garlic cloves, finely chopped
1 pound 2 ounces boneless, skinless chicken thighs, roughly chopped
1 red chili, seeded and finely sliced
1 tablespoon fish sauce
a pinch of sugar
juice of ½ lime
2½ cups hot chicken stock
rice, to serve

GOES WELL WITH
Char Kueh Toew (Fried Rice Noodles with Shrimp and Egg) (page 193)

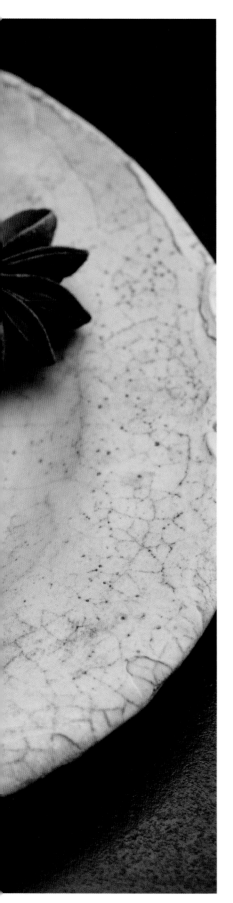

Star Anise

Well, star anise definitely wins the prize for being the best-looking spice. This beautiful mahogany-colored, dried fruit has eight petallike compartments that each store a tiny, shiny seed.

Star anise is actually the unripened fruit of a small tree that is native to China, which is still the major producer of the spice today. Its name in Chinese means "eight quarters," although, like a magic clover, you can find lucky twelve-pointed ones. The smell and taste is intense aniseed, which lends itself to so many different cuisines around the world. Star anise is one of the major components in Chinese five spice and is one of the "big" flavors used in any slow-braised meat dishes. In Indian cooking, it is ground into a powder and mixed with other spices to make garam masala. In Vietnam, the aniseed flavor adds a fresh note to the stock of their prized national soup dish *Pho*. In the West, star anise is often used in fusion cooking, and it works particularly well in a sugar syrup drizzled over poached pears or peaches.

Star anise is generally bought whole and added to hot oil, stocks and sauces to impart its flavor. In a dry, airtight container, which is kept out of direct sunlight, the spice will last more than a year. The best indication of its freshness is the smell; once this starts to fade so does the flavor, and at that point you know it's time to go and get some more.

Char-Grilled Cilantro and Mint Chicken

SERVES 4
1 pound 2 ounces boneless, skinless
    chicken thighs
olive oil, for brushing

FOR THE MARINADE
1 large handful mint leaves
1 large handful cilantro leaves
1 green chili, seeded and roughly
    chopped
1¼ cups plain yogurt
2 teaspoons garam masala
juice of 1 lemon
sea salt

GOES WELL WITH
Shrimp and Lemongrass Rice Noodle
    Salad (page 46)
Malay Yellow Mussel Curry
    (page 142)

1 To make the marinade, put all the ingredients into a food processor and blend until smooth. Reserve half of the mixture to use as a sauce later and mix the rest with the chicken in a large mixing bowl until the chicken is completely coated. Cover and leave to marinate in the refrigerator 30 minutes, or overnight if time allows.

2 Wipe the marinade off the chicken thighs to stop them burning, then rub a little oil on both sides of all the pieces of chicken. Heat a griddle pan, or skillet if you don't have one, until smoking, then cook the chicken 5 to 6 minutes each side until golden and cooked through.

3 Slice the chicken into strips and serve immediately, with the reserved yogurt mixture spooned over.

Moroccan Cinnamon and Lemon Chicken

1 Preheat the oven to 375°F. Heat the oil in a Dutch oven over medium heat, then add the onion and cinnamon. Cook, stirring occasionally, 6 to 7 minutes until the onion is just turning golden.

2 Add the tomatoes, turmeric and black pepper and season with a good pinch of salt. Mix everything together well and then add the chicken. Cover the chicken with alternate layers of potato and lemon slices (the order doesn't matter), then pour enough freshly boiled water over to just cover everything. Put the Dutch oven in the oven with the lid on, then cook 1 hour, or until the chicken is cooked through and beautifully tender.

3 Return the Dutch oven to the stovetop over medium heat, remove the lid and simmer 15 minutes, stirring occasionally and very gently, so the sauce reduces. Gently stir in the parsley and serve immediately.

SERVES 4
2 tablespoons olive oil
1 onion, roughly sliced
1-inch piece cinnamon stick
2 large tomatoes, roughly chopped
½ teaspoon turmeric
¼ teaspoon freshly ground black pepper
3 pounds 5 ounces chicken legs and
    thighs on the bone, skinned
2 cups roughly sliced small waxy
    potatoes
1 unwaxed lemon, thinly sliced and
    seeds removed
2 large handfuls parsley leaves, finely
    chopped
sea salt

GOES WELL WITH
Fattoush Salad (see page 33)
Charred Eggplants with Indian Spices
    and Cilantro (page 161)
Vanilla and Honey Syllabub
    (page 202)

Kerala Korma

I discovered this wonderful take on the classic korma in the hills of Kerala in South India. When I was young, my parents often fed me and my siblings kormas, a mild curry, as a way of "breaking us in" to the delights of more heavily spiced curries. As my taste for all things spicy grew, I left this introductory curry behind and moved on to a new world of curried delights. This modern recipe is definitely a reason to revisit the korma. Fresh, savory and with a background heat from the chili, it's a million miles away from the sweet, bland curry that is served up in too many local Indian restaurants.

SERVES 4
2 cups coconut cream
⅓ cup cashew nuts
1-inch piece gingerroot, peeled
½ green chili, seeded
1 teaspoon ground coriander
½ teaspoon ground cumin
1½ teaspoons sea salt
2 tablespoons vegetable oil
1 large onion, finely chopped
a large pinch of fresh curry leaves
1 pound 2 ounces boneless, skinless
   chicken thighs, thinly sliced
juice of 1 lime
rice, to serve

GOES WELL WITH
Indian Spinach Cutlets with Raita
   (page 163)
Red Lentil Dal (page 174)

1 Put the coconut cream, cashew nuts, ginger, green chili, coriander, cumin and salt into a food processor and blend to a smooth sauce.

2 Heat the oil in a saucepan over medium heat, then add the onion and cook, stirring occasionally, 6 to 8 minutes until the onion turns golden. Pour in the coconut sauce, mix well and cook over medium heat 1 minute, stirring continuously, then add the curry leaves.

3 Add the chicken and lime juice and bring to a boil. Cover, reduce the heat to low and simmer 12 to 15 minutes until the chicken is cooked through and tender and the sauce thick. If its gets too thick and gloopy, add a little hot water to loosen it up. Serve immediately with rice.

Indian Chicken and Spinach Curry

Everywhere I went in India there was a different take on this classic curry: sometimes the main ingredient was lamb and sometimes the Indian cheese *paneer* (a great substitute if you're vegetarian.) For my version, I use chicken and get the blender to do most of the work, so it's nice and easy. If you want a healthy version, leave out the cream—it still tastes superb.

SERVES 4

10 ounces baby spinach
1½ teaspoons garam masala
1 teaspoon sea salt
1 large onion, roughly chopped
2 tomatoes, quartered
4 garlic cloves
1-inch piece gingerroot, peeled and roughly chopped
½ green chili, seeded
2 tablespoons vegetable oil
2 teaspoons cumin seeds
1 pound 2 ounces boneless, skinless chicken thighs, cut into bite-size pieces
¼ cup heavy cream (optional)

GOES WELL WITH

Gobi Masala (Indian Stir-Fried Cauliflower) (page 172)
Herb and Spice Pilaf Rice (page 181)

1 Bring a large saucepan, half-filled with water, to a boil and add the spinach. Cook 1 to 2 minutes until just wilting, then strain, reserving the cooking water. Put the spinach and a scant ½ cup of the cooking water into a food processor or blender and puree until smooth. If using an upright blender, remember to leave a tiny gap in the lid for the steam to escape. Transfer the spinach to a bowl and set aside to cool.

2 Using the same food processor (don't worry about washing it), blend the garam masala, salt, onion, tomatoes, garlic, ginger, green chili and a little water until smooth.

3 Heat the oil in a large saucepan over medium heat and throw in the cumin seeds. Wait 10 seconds until they start crackling, then pour in the tomato mixture. Give it a good stir, cover, reduce the heat to low and simmer 30 minutes, stirring occasionally.

4 Tip in the spinach, chicken and cream, if using, and stir well. Turn the heat up to medium-high and cook, stirring occasionally, 12 to 15 minutes until the chicken is cooked through and tender.

Bangkok Garlic and Black Pepper Chicken

I love to find food inspiration everywhere I go, and I would love to say that I first tried this stir-fry sitting on a *mon khwon* (Thai triangle cushion) on the beach watching the sun set over the Gulf of Thailand, or huddled at a tiny plastic table at the famous Chatuchak market. Sadly not: I ate this in the sterile surroundings of a food hall in a huge Bangkok shopping mall. But no matter—this is still an incredible dish. Don't be scared about the crazy-seeming amount of garlic; cooking it first mellows the flavor so you're left with something that's sweet, sticky and not too pungent.

SERVES 4

4 tablespoons vegetable oil
8 garlic cloves, very roughly sliced
1 pound 2 ounces boneless, skinless
    chicken breasts, cut into very thin
    strips
2 teaspoons freshly ground black pepper
1 tablespoon fish sauce
a pinch of sugar
juice of 1 lime

GOES WELL WITH

Veracruz Rice with Seafood
    (page 178)
Mango, Orange and Nutmeg
    Cheesecake (page 201)

1   Heat a wok over high heat and add the oil. When the oil is hot, stir-fry the garlic 20 to 30 seconds until just turning golden, then remove with a slotted spoon and place on paper towels. Watch the garlic carefully while it's cooking—if it starts to change color quickly, remove the wok from the heat immediately so the garlic doesn't burn. You want the garlic to be golden on the outside and tender and sweet inside.

2   Pour off half the oil from the wok and reheat the remainder over high heat. Add the chicken and stir-fry 3 to 4 minutes until it is golden, cooked through and tender.

3   Add the black pepper, fish sauce, sugar, lime juice and cooked garlic. Mix everything together and serve immediately.

Chicken in Macadamia Nut and Mustard Seed Sauce

1 To make the spice paste, put all the ingredients into a mini food processor with 2 tablespoons water and blend until smooth.

2 Heat a wok over high heat and add the oil. Once smoking, add the onion and stir-fry 3 to 4 minutes until golden. Tip in the mustard seeds and stir-fry 30 seconds, or until they start popping in the oil. Spoon in the spice paste and stir-fry 30 seconds longer, or until fragrant.

3 Reduce the heat to medium and add the chicken, soy sauce, white wine vinegar and ¼ cup freshly boiled water. Mix well and cook, stirring occasionally, 10 to 12 minutes until the chicken is cooked through and tender and the sauce is really thick. Scatter the cilantro over and serve immediately with rice.

SERVES 4
2 tablespoons vegetable oil
1 onion, roughly chopped
2 teaspoons black mustard seeds
1 pound 2 ounces boneless, skinless chicken thighs, cut into bite-size pieces
2 tablespoons soy sauce
1 tablespoon white wine vinegar
chopped cilantro leaves, to serve
rice, to serve

FOR THE SPICE PASTE
⅓ cup unsalted macadamia nuts
2 red chilies, seeded
1-inch piece gingerroot, peeled and roughly chopped
2 teaspoons ground coriander
½ teaspoon turmeric

GOES WELL WITH
Broiled Monkfish Salad with a Red Pepper, Roasted Garlic and Chili Dressing (page 50)
Nasi Goreng (Indonesian Fried Rice) (page 186)

Mexican Chicken with Yogurt and Almonds

1   Heat the oil in a Dutch oven over high heat. Add the chicken thighs and cook, skin-side down, 3 to 4 minutes until the skin turns a lovely golden color. Turn the chicken thighs over, chuck in the garlic and cook 30 seconds longer, or until fragrant. Pour in the stock and bring to a boil. Cover, reduce the heat to low and simmer gently 20 minutes, or until the chicken is just cooked through and tender.

2   Meanwhile, heat a medium skillet over medium-high heat. Add the jalapeño chilies and red peppers. Char them, turning occasionally, 3 to 4 minutes until they develop a few really blackened areas. This provides the lovely smoky flavor so typical of Mexican cooking. Once cool enough to touch, skin and seed the chilies and remove any really charred bits from the peppers. Thinly slice the pieces of pepper and the chilies.

3   Put the almonds into a food processor and pulse a few times. You want the almonds to be fairly well ground, but still retain some chunky texture.

4   Bring the chicken back to a boil over medium heat, then add the chilies, peppers, almonds, scallions and orange juice and season with a really good pinch of salt and pepper. Mix everything together so it is well combined and cook 10 minutes.

5   Add the yogurt, reduce the heat to low and simmer gently, stirring occasionally, 10 minutes longer, or until the sauce is like a lovely thick soup. Serve immediately with tortilla chips on the side.

SERVES 4

2 tablespoons olive oil
4 chicken thighs on the bone,
    5½ to 7ounces each
2 garlic cloves, finely chopped
1¼ cups chicken stock
2 red jalapeño chilies
2 red bell peppers, seeded and cut into
    8 pieces each
⅓ cup blanched almonds
4 scallions, finely chopped
juice of 1 orange
1 cup plus 2 tablespoons thick
    Greek-style yogurt
sea salt and freshly ground black pepper
tortilla chips, to serve

GOES WELL WITH
Feta, Walnut and Nigella Seed Salad
    (page 21)
Veracruz Rice with Seafood
    (page 178)
Mayan Hot Chocolate (page 213)

Cumin

The wonderful spice that is cumin is used all over the world in so many different ways, from flavoring cheese to making curries—everyone loves it. This is because cumin has such a lovely earthy flavor, and the little ridged seeds are full of essential oils that give it a pungent aroma that always takes me back to the Media of Fez every time.

When you cook with cumin you either use it whole or ground. The seeds are generally added to hot oil at the start of the cooking process, adding a nutty flavor to the finished dish. Ground cumin can be used in loads of different ways and is an essential ingredient in most curry powders.

You will often hear chefs talking about dry roasting spices before grinding them into a powder. What they mean by this is adding the seeds to a skillet, without any oil, and gently toasting them over low heat, shaking the pan as you go, until you are literally hit by the smell of the spice. The heat coaxes out the fragrant essential oils in the seeds and this enhances the flavor of the spices. Always allow roasted spices to cool down completely before you grind them into a powder, otherwise they won't break down properly.

When you cook with cumin, or any spice, it likes a bit of loving. The seeds can burn easily, which makes them taste bitter. To avoid this, when you are dry roasting any spice, keep the heat low, shake the pan from time to time and keep an eye on them; their smell will let you know when they are ready.

Ground cumin will last about six months and whole cumin seeds will last very nicely for about a year. Both are best stored in a dry, airtight container out of direct sunlight.

Kadahi Chicken

I love that a curry can be so fresh, healthy and exciting, and my chicken kadahi is proof that you don't need more than five spices to make a curry really spectacular. The cumin seeds provide a wonderful, nutty spice base and the simple flavors of the garlic, ginger, garam masala and turmeric work together to provide everything else. The lemon juice freshens the curry and brings out the flavors of the spices even more.

SERVES 4

2 tablespoons vegetable oil
2 teaspoons cumin seeds
1 large onion, finely chopped
1 green chili, seeded and finely chopped
1-inch piece gingerroot, peeled and finely chopped
4 tomatoes, roughly chopped
1 teaspoon garam masala
½ teaspoon turmeric
1½ teaspoons salt
1 pound 2 ounces boneless, skinless chicken thighs, cut into thin strips
1 green bell pepper, seeded and cut into thin strips
juice of ½ lemon
rice, to serve (optional)

GOES WELL WITH
Roasted Cambodian Eggplants with Ginger and Coconut (page 170)
Red Lentil Dal (page 174)

1 Heat a wok over medium heat and add the oil. Chuck in the cumin seeds, allow them to crackle 10 seconds, then add the onion. Stir-fry 3 to 4 minutes until the onion starts turning golden, then add the green chili, ginger, tomatoes, garam masala, turmeric and salt. Mix well and stir-fry 5 to 6 minutes until the tomatoes are breaking down and form a sauce.

2 Add the chicken and green pepper, reduce the heat to low and simmer, stirring occasionally, 12 to 15 minutes until the chicken is cooked through and tender. Add the lemon juice and give it one last mix. Serve immediately with rice, if liked.

Rosamma's Crispy Chili Chicken

SERVES 4

3 pounds 5 ounces chicken legs and
    thighs on the bone, skinned
2 tablespoons vegetable oil, plus about
    1½ cups for shallow frying
1 large onion, finely chopped
2 tablespoons all-purpose flour
a large pinch dried curry leaves
juice of ½ lemon

FOR THE SPICE PASTE

8 garlic cloves
1-inch piece gingerroot, peeled
2 teaspoons mild chili powder
¼ teaspoon turmeric
1½ teaspoons sea salt
2 tablespoons white wine vinegar

GOES WELL WITH

Red Lentil Dal (page 174)
Sri Lankan Fried Potatoes
    (page 166)
Steamed Ginger Custard Pots
    (page 199)

1. Put the spice paste ingredients in a mini food processor and blend until smooth. Transfer to a large mixing bowl, then add the chicken and mix until the chicken is completely coated. Cover and set aside to marinate 30 minutes, or overnight in the refrigerator if time allows.

2. Heat 2 tablespoons of oil in a large skillet or wok over medium heat, then add the onion and stir-fry 6 to 8 minutes until golden. Add the chicken, any remaining curry paste and 2½ cups boiling water, which should be just enough to cover everything. Bring to a boil, then reduce the heat to low and simmer, stirring occasionally, 40 to 45 minutes until the chicken is cooked through and tender and the sauce reduces by about half.

3. Remove the pan from the heat, lift out the chicken pieces to a plate, using a slotted spoon, and set both the liquid and chicken pieces to one side. When the chicken is cool enough to handle, dust each piece with a little flour. Heat the oil for shallow frying in a deep skillet over medium heat—you want the oil to half cover the chicken pieces. Once small bubbles start appearing in the oil, shallow fry the chicken in batches of 3 or 4 pieces 2 to 3 minutes on each side until golden and crisp. Remove the chicken with a slotted spoon and place on paper towels.

4. Pour the liquid from the chicken into a skillet or wok over medium heat bring to a boil. Rub the curry leaves between your hands so they break up and then scatter into the pan. Cook 10 to 12 minutes until the mixture is really thick and sticky, stirring regularly so nothing burns, especially as the sauce starts to thicken.

5. Add the chicken and mix everything together until the chicken is well coated in the rich, sticky sauce. Serve immediately, squeezing the lemon juice over to freshen things up and bring out all the lovely flavors even more.

Thai Red Duck Curry

1 Remove the duck breasts from the refrigerator at least 30 minutes before cooking, so they are not too cold to cook perfectly in the middle.

2 To prepare the curry paste, remove the really tough outer leaves from the lemongrass and cut off the ends of the stalks. Starting at the fatter end, roughly slice each lemongrass stalk into rings. You should see a purple band in the rings. Stop slicing when there are no more purple bands and discard the rest of the lemongrass, as it will be too tough to eat. Put the chopped lemongrass in a mini food processor with the other curry paste ingredients and blend until smooth.

3 Heat 2 tablespoons of the oil in a large wok over medium heat. Add the curry paste and fry, stirring continuously, 30 seconds, or until fragrant. Pour in the coconut milk, fish sauce and lime juice and mix well. Turn the heat up to high and bring to a boil, then reduce the heat to low and simmer, stirring occasionally, 10 minutes, or until the sauce reduces slightly.

4 Heat the remaining oil in a large skillet over medium heat. Carefully add the duck breasts and cook 6 to 7 minutes on each side until they are golden on the outside but slightly pink in the middle. Remove the duck breasts from the pan and leave to cool a little, then cut into bite-size pieces.

5 Tip the duck into the wok with the curry sauce, stir gently and cook over medium heat 2 to 3 minutes so the duck absorbs the wonderful flavors of the spices and coconut milk. Serve immediately with rice.

SERVES 4

4 skinless duck breasts, 6 to 7 ounces each
4 tablespoons vegetable oil
1¾ cups coconut milk
2 tablespoons fish sauce
juice of ½ lime
rice, to serve

FOR THE CURRY PASTE

2 lemongrass stalks
¼ cup roasted, unsalted peanuts
2 red chilies, seeded
2 teaspoons ground coriander
1 teaspoon ground cumin
½ teaspoon coarsely ground black pepper

GOES WELL WITH

Jetalah Pineapple, Cucumber and Chili Salad (page 30)
Tomato and Coconut Rice (page 187)

Pueblan Almond Duck

SERVES 4

4 duck breasts, skin on, 6 to 7 ounces
   each
5 tablespoons olive oil
4 tomatoes, roughly chopped
1 ounce French bread, roughly torn
   into bite-size pieces (scant ¼ cup)
⅓ cup almonds
2-inch piece cinnamon stick
6 whole cloves
2 dried red chilies
1¼ cups chicken stock
sea salt and freshly ground black pepper
slivered almonds, toasted, to serve

GOES WELL WITH

Pomegranate, Fennel, Orange and
   Watercress Salad (page 22)
Veracruz Rice with Seafood
   (page 178)
Cambodian Caramelized Ginger
   Bananas with Vanilla Ice Cream
   (page 212)

1 Remove the duck breasts from the refrigerator at least 30 minutes before cooking, so they are not too cold to cook perfectly in the middle.

2 Heat 3 tablespoons of the oil in a large saucepan over medium heat, then add the tomatoes, French bread, almonds, cinnamon, cloves and dried red chilies. Give everything a good stir, so it all gets coated in the oil. Fry 4 to 5 minutes until the tomatoes start to break down, stirring occasionally so nothing burns. Pour the tomato mixture into a food processor with scant 1 cup water and blend 4 to 5 minutes until smooth.

3 Pour back into the pan and add the stock, stir well and bring to a boil over high heat. Reduce the heat to low and simmer gently 25 minutes, partially covered. This allows the liquid to reduce slightly and the flavors to develop.

4 Season the duck breasts on both sides with a little salt and pepper. Heat the remaining 2 tablespoons of oil in a large skillet over medium heat, then cook the duck breasts 5 to 6 minutes on each side until they are golden on the outside but still pink in the middle. Remove the duck breasts from the pan, slice into 3 or 4 pieces and then return to the pan.

5 Reheat the sauce, then pour over the duck breasts. Leave to rest 5 minutes, then serve scattered with the slivered almonds.

CHAPTER THREE

Meat

This chapter really showcases how you can create a variety of really inspiring and mouth-watering dishes with just a few of the right spices. There is something for everyone here—delicious tacos, succulent kebabs, spicy stir-frys, rich curries, fragrant stews, stuffed peppers, delicate char-grills and sophisticated roasts. If you are new to cooking with spices the Stir-Fried Beef with Black Pepper and Basil is an incredible dish to start with. It's so simple, only relying on black pepper to give it all the heat and background flavor you need. It always amazes me what you can do with only few basic cupboard spices. The depth of flavor that comes from cumin, coriander, cinnamon and nutmeg, as used in the melt-in-the-mouth Lebanese Leg of Lamb with Spiced Lentil Puree, is a perfect example.

LEFT: Al Pastor Pork and Pineapple Salad (page 110)

Shredded Beef Tacos

SERVES 4

1 pound 2 ounces braising or skirt steak
2 tablespoons olive oil
1 small onion, finely chopped
3 garlic cloves, finely chopped
4 tomatoes, finely chopped
½ teaspoon dried oregano
½ teaspoon dried thyme
1 green jalapeño chili, seeded and finely
    chopped
1 tablespoon white wine vinegar
    or apple cider vinegar
1 tablespoon tomato paste
a pinch of sugar
8 small flour tortillas, broiled (optional)
scant 1 cup sour cream
1 small romaine lettuce, shredded
4 radishes, thinly sliced
3 ounces feta cheese
sea salt and freshly ground black pepper

GOES WELL WITH

Frijoles Negros (Mexican Refried
    Beans with Garlic, Chilies and
    Cilantro) (page 175)
Vanilla and Honey Syllabub
    (page 202)

1 Bring a large saucepan of water to a boil. Add the beef, turn the heat down to low and simmer 30 minutes, or until the beef is cooked through. Remove the beef from the water and set to aside to cool.

2 Meanwhile, heat the oil in a large saucepan over medium heat. Add the onion and garlic and cook, stirring occasionally, 6 to 8 minutes until the onion is lovely and golden. Add the tomatoes, oregano, thyme, green jalapeño chili, vinegar, tomato paste and sugar and season with a really good pinch of salt and pepper. Reduce the heat to low, cover and cook 20 minutes, then remove the lid and cook, stirring occasionally, 10 minutes longer, or until the mixture gets really thick.

3 Flake the cooked beef into small pieces and add to the pan with the tomato sauce. Mix well, turn the heat up to medium and cook 3 to 4 minutes until the beef is hot all the way through.

4 To assemble the tacos, place a good tablespoonful of beef into the middle of each tortilla with a generous dollop of sour cream. Scatter some lettuce, radishes and feta over. Roll up or leave open, as you like, and serve immediately.

Fried Steaks with Black Pepper Dip

This peppery, Cambodian-inspired dipping sauce goes perfectly with the juicy steak. My favorite steak is a rib-eye, brought to room temperature and cooked really quickly so it's nice and rare, but you can use any of the different cuts you like and cook them whichever way you prefer.

SERVES 4
4 rib-eye steaks, about 9 ounces each
2 tablespoons olive oil
sea salt and freshly ground black pepper

FOR THE DIPPING SAUCE
2 garlic cloves, roughly chopped
1 teaspoon sea salt
1 teaspoon freshly ground black pepper
½ teaspoon sugar
juice of 1 lemon
1 tablespoon oyster sauce

GOES WELL WITH
Chinese Tiger Salad (page 26)
Shrimp and Lemongrass Rice Noodle
    Salad (page 46)
Dark Chocolate, Clove and Cinnamon
    Brownies (page 196)

1   Remove the steaks from the refrigerator at least 20 minutes before cooking, so they are not too cold to cook evenly. Season both sides with a good pinch of salt and pepper.

2   To make the dipping sauce, blend the garlic and salt to a paste in a mini food processor. Alternatively, you can sprinkle the salt over the garlic cloves and crush them with the back of a knife, rubbing until they form a paste. Put the paste in a small bowl with the rest of the dipping sauce ingredients, add 1 tablespoon water and mix well. Set aside at least 10 minutes to let the flavors develop.

3   Heat a skillet over high heat, add the oil and fry the steaks 1 minute 30 seconds to 2 minutes 30 seconds each side. Don't touch them for at least the first 1 minute 30 seconds of cooking, as this lets a lovely golden crust to form.

4   Set the steaks aside 5 minutes to rest, then serve with the dipping sauce.

Stir-Fried Beef with Black Pepper and Basil

Salt and pepper grace most kitchen tables as a seasoning, but don't forget that pepper is the king of spices and used generously it provides the most fragrant, warm heat that works perfectly with beef. Add garlic and ginger for a freshness and balsamic vinegar for a sour, modern twist, and you have a stir-fry really worth talking about.

1   Heat a wok over high heat and add the oil. Once the oil is hot, add the sliced beef and stir-fry 1 to 2 minutes until turning golden.
2   Add the garlic, ginger and black pepper and stir-fry for another minute, then add the sugar, soy sauce, balsamic vinegar and basil leaves. Mix well and serve immediately.

SERVES 4
2 tablespoons vegetable oil
1 pound 2 ounces beef tenderloin, thinly sliced
4 garlic cloves, finely chopped
1-inch piece gingerroot, peeled and finely chopped
2 teaspoons freshly ground black pepper
a pinch of sugar
1 tablespoon light soy sauce
1 tablespoon balsamic vinegar
1 large handful basil leaves, roughly torn

GOES WELL WITH
Rosamma's Crispy Chili Chicken (page 80)
Beijing Teahouse Vegetable Stir-fry (page 169)
Steamed Ginger Custard Pots (page 199)

Black Pepper

You can't have a spice book without talking about black pepper. We all know it, we all use it and this has been the case for a very long time. The spicy pungency of pepper is exactly why people have loved it for so long; in the past it flavored bland food with its wonderful kick. Salted meat was made palatable with pepper, hence the modern-day pairing of salt and pepper as a seasoning.

Pepper is native to the Malabar Coast of India, where it has been exported for thousands of years. The Indians, who never miss a food trick, have loved this precious spice since 2000 B.C. The ancient Greeks and Romans began to import the spice from India to add a kick to their food, and after the decline of the Roman empire, the Persians and Arabs traded the valuable spice with Europe. It was an instant success, and its importance played a great part in shaping the modern world today. The European ports of Venice and Genoa boomed and, in a quest to source new trade routes for this valuable commodity, Christopher Columbus discovered a little place called America!

Pepper comes in lots of different varieties: black, green, white, red and even pink. Apart from the pink, however, they all come from the same plant. The green pepper is the unripened berry, which turns red when ripe and then goes black when dried— the pepper we know and love. When gently pickled, the husk is removed and the berry turns white.

The beautiful pepper berries grow in neat little bunches on vines that attach themselves to host trees in the tropical forests. While traveling, I was really lucky to be in Kerala while the pepper harvest was in full swing. My friend Manu took me around his beautiful organic spice farm, where the pepper vines wound their way up the tallest jackfruit trees. The pepper pickers climbed the trees, with no ladders, and picked the precious crop, which was then left to dry in little piles in the afternoon sun.

Estella's Mexican Beef-Filled Peppers with a Pecan Sauce

SERVES 4

2 tablespoons olive oil, plus extra
for drizzling
1 large onion, finely chopped
9 ounces ground beef
2 garlic cloves, finely chopped
1 teaspoon ground cumin
¼ teaspoon ground cloves
½ teaspoon chili flakes
¼ cup almonds, roughly chopped
4 tomatoes, finely chopped
1 cup beef stock
1 handful cilantro leaves, finely
chopped, plus extra to serve
2 red bell peppers, halved lengthwise
and seeded
sea salt and freshly ground black pepper

FOR THE SAUCE

½ cup pecan nuts, plus extra to serve
(optional)
⅔ cup sour cream

GOES WELL WITH

Jetalah Pineapple, Cucumber and Chili
Salad (page 30)
Mango, Orange and Nutmeg
Cheesecake (page 201)

1 Preheat the oven to 375°F. Heat the oil in a large skillet over medium heat, then add the onion and cook, stirring occasionally, 6 to 8 minutes until the onion turns golden. Add the ground beef, garlic, cumin, cloves, chilli flakes, almonds, tomatoes and stock and season with a really good pinch of salt and pepper. Mix well and cook for about 10 minutes until the beef is cooked through and the sauce reduces down so it's really thick. Throw in the cilantro and mix well.

2 Spoon the beef mixture into the pepper halves, drizzle with a little olive oil and bake 20 to 25 minutes until the peppers are soft and starting to turn golden brown.

3 Meanwhile, put all the sauce ingredients into a food processor with a splash of water and blend until completely smooth. Drizzle over the sweet, juicy stuffed peppers, sprinkle with a little chopped cilantro and serve immediately. Alternatively, serve the sauce on the side, scattered with chopped pecans.

Ciya Shish Kebabs

These kebabs are completely delicious—juicy meat with crunchy nuts, oozing cheese, lovely sour sumac, loads of fresh herbs and crisp tortilla bread. Traditionally, the kebabs are cooked over charcoal using huge metal skewers, but I just use a pair of tongs to turn the meat under the broiler. Feel free to use a skewer if you like.

SERVES 4

14 ounces ground beef
1 teaspoon ground cumin
2 tablespoons olive oil, plus extra for brushing
1 cup plain yogurt
4 flour tortillas
½ cup roughly chopped walnuts
4 ounces fresh mozzarella, drained and roughly sliced
1 handful parsley leaves, finely chopped
1 handful mint leaves, finely chopped
4 scallions, finely sliced
1 teaspoon sumac, plus extra to serve
lemon wedges, to serve
sea salt and freshly ground black pepper

GOES WELL WITH

Char-Grilled Halloumi, Tomato and
  Olive Salad (page 18)
Guacamole and Shrimp Salad
  (page 42)

1 Preheat the broiler to high. In a large mixing bowl, season the ground beef with a really good pinch of salt and pepper, then add the cumin and mix well. Divide the seasoned ground beef into 8 equal portions, roll out into 5½-inch-long sausage shapes and brush with a little oil. Place the kebabs under the hot broiler and broil 3 to 4 minutes on each side, or until they are just turning brown and are cooked through and tender.

2 Place a tablespoon of yogurt in the middle of each tortilla and spread out with the back of a spoon. Sprinkle a quarter of the walnuts, mozzarella, parsley, mint and scallions over each tortilla, then sprinkle each with a pinch of sumac, salt and pepper. Place 2 cooked kebabs on top and roll the tortilla up tightly, tucking in the side as you go.

3 Heat the oil in a skillet over medium heat, then fry the kebabs 1 minute on each side, or until they turn golden and crisp. Slice the kebabs in half and serve immediately with the remaining yogurt, sprinkled with sumac and with lemon wedges for squeezing over.

Roast Lebanese Leg of Lamb with Spiced Lentil Puree

1 Put the cumin, coriander, cinnamon, nutmeg and oil in a large mixing bowl, then add a good pinch of salt and mix well. Add the lamb to the bowl and rub in the paste until the lamb is well coated. Cover with plastic wrap and set aside at least 2 hours, or overnight in the refrigerator if time allows.

2 Preheat the oven to 400°F, leaving a broiler tray in the oven to heat up. Carefully place the seasoned lamb onto the hot broiler tray, skin side up, and roast 30 to 35 minutes until the lamb is beautifully colored and crisp on the outside and juicy and pink in the middle. Remove from the oven, squeeze the lemon juice over and season with a good pinch of salt. Cover with foil and leave to rest 10 minutes so the meat becomes even more tender and delicious.

3 Meanwhile, cook the lentils in a large pan of boiling water 12 to 15 minutes until they are cooked through and soft. Drain and set aside.

4 Heat the oil in a large saucepan over medium heat, then add the onion and garlic and gently fry, stirring occasionally, 6 to 8 minutes until golden. Throw in the cumin and coriander and cook 30 seconds, stirring frequently, or until fragrant. Add the cooked lentils, lemon juice and 1 cup freshly boiled water and season with a really good pinch of salt and pepper. Use a hand blender to puree the lentils until they are lovely and smooth, adding a little more water if the mixture gets too thick. Scatter in the parsley and gently mix to combine.

5 Finely slice the lamb and divide between the serving plates. Spoon any juices from the broiler tray over, add a good dollop of the lentil puree to the top of the lamb and a drizzle of oil, then serve immediately.

SERVES 4 TO 6

1 tablespoon ground cumin
2 teaspoons ground coriander
½ teaspoon ground cinnamon
a pinch of grated nutmeg
4 tablespoons olive oil, plus extra
    for drizzling
1 lamb leg, about 3½ pounds,
    butterflied
juice of ½ lemon
sea salt

FOR THE LENTIL PUREE

1 cup green lentils, washed and drained
2 tablespoons olive oil
1 onion, finely chopped
2 garlic cloves, finely chopped
1 teaspoon ground cumin
1 teaspoon ground coriander
juice of 1 lemon
1 handful parsley leaves, finely chopped
sea salt and freshly ground black pepper

GOES WELL WITH

Pomegranate, Fennel, Orange and
    Watercress Salad (page 22)

Golden Temple Lamb Curry

This lamb curry is inspired by the wonderful food I ate in Amritsar in Northwest India. The city is home to the beautiful Golden Temple, the holiest place in the world for Sikhs, and one of the most incredible places I have ever been to. The best food I ate in India was always in someone's house, and in Amritsar I was lucky enough to spend most of my time with my lovely friend Nitya's family, who made sure I never went hungry. This is my take on the delicious classic Punjabi cuisine I enjoyed at their home.

SERVES 4

3 tomatoes, roughly chopped
1-inch piece gingerroot, peeled
    and roughly chopped
3 garlic cloves
2 teaspoons mild chili powder
1½ teaspoons garam masala
1 teaspoon ground cumin
2 teaspoons sea salt
2 tablespoons vegetable oil
2 red onions, finely chopped
1 pound 2 ounces lamb leg, cut into
    1-inch cubes
1 large handful cilantro leaves,
    to serve

GOES WELL WITH

Cambodian Roasted Eggplants with
    Ginger and Coconut (page 170)
Sri Lankan Fried Rice with Cashew
    Nuts and Egg (page 182)

1   Put the tomatoes, ginger, garlic, chili powder, garam masala, cumin and salt into a food processor with 1 tablespoon water and blend until smooth.

2   Heat the oil in a large saucepan over medium heat, then add the onions and cook, stirring occasionally, 6 to 8 minutes until they turn golden.

3   Pour the blended tomato mixture into the pan with the onions, then add the lamb and enough hot water to just cover everything. Give it all a good mix, cover and cook 1 hour 30 minutes, remembering to stir occasionally.

4   Remove the lamb from the heat and set aside 5 minutes to let the meat rest and become even more juicy and tender. Sprinkle loads of cilantro leaves over and serve immediately.

Dongbei Cumin and Cilantro Stir-Fried Lamb

Lamb and cumin weren't my idea of the classic ingredients I thought I'd be sampling in China, but I found them together on the menu of an amazing Dongbei restaurant in Shanghai. Dongbei is in the northeast of China, and is known for its harsh, below-freezing winters. The food from this region tends to be warming, hearty and spicy, and has been influenced by Korean, Mongolian, Japanese and even Russian cuisines. The food at Dongbei was delicious; in fact, we ordered so much that the staff were laughing at us. They brought out dish after dish and then, when I was ready to give up, out came the lamb. It was so special I ordered more rice and ate the lot! The staff were impressed and gave us free shots of the local spirit *baijiu*, which is 60 percent alcohol! Luckily, I could still remember the recipe afterward...

1 Finely chop the cilantro stems, which are full of flavor, and roughly chop the leaves, which add a lovely crunch to the dish.

2 Heat a wok over high heat and add the oil. Once smoking hot, chuck in the cumin seeds, dried red chilies and garlic, then stir-fry 10 seconds, or until fragrant. Add the lamb and stir-fry 3 to 4 minutes until the lamb starts to brown.

3 Pour in the soy sauce, add the sugar and stir-fry 10 seconds, then throw in the cilantro. Mix well and serve immediately with rice.

SERVES 4
2 large handfuls cilantro sprigs
2 tablespoons vegetable oil
2 teaspoons cumin seeds
2 dried red chilies, roughly chopped
3 garlic cloves, finely chopped
1 pound 2 ounces lamb steaks, tenderloin or boned loin chops, thinly sliced
2 tablespoons light soy sauce
a pinch of sugar
rice, to serve

GOES WELL WITH
Chinese Pork Dumpling Soup
(page 15)

Persian Saffron and Honey Lamb Stew

The earthy smell of saffron evokes the windy souks, sweet mint teas, colorful spice markets and beautiful mosques that inspired me to make this wonderful Persian stew. The saffron and cinnamon are all you need to provide a real depth of flavor and the honey and apricots lend just the right amount of sweetness, which works perfectly with the lamb. This stew is rich but light and full of flavor from such amazing spices.

1 Season the meat with a really good pinch of salt and pepper. Heat the oil in a large Dutch oven over medium heat, then add the lamb in batches and cook, turning occasionally, 10 minutes, or until brown all over. Remove with a slotted spoon and set aside.

2 Add the onion to the pan and stir-fry 3 to 4 minutes until it starts to turn golden. Return the lamb to the pan and add the chickpeas, saffron, cinnamon and 2½ cups freshly boiled water, which should be enough to just cover everything. Season with a good pinch of salt and pepper and gently mix together. Bring to a boil and cover, then reduce the heat to low and simmer 1 hour, or until the meat is cooked through and tender.

3 Add the honey and apricots, increase the heat to medium and cook, uncovered, stirring occasionally, 20 minutes, or until the sauce reduces a little.

4 Remove the Dutch oven from the heat, cover and set aside 5 to 10 minutes for the stew to rest a little before it is served. Pour the lemon juice over, then scatter the parsley over and serve immediately with steamed rice.

SERVES 4

1 pound 2 ounces lamb leg, cut into 1-inch cubes
2 tablespoons olive oil
1 large onion, finely chopped
1 can (15-oz.) chickpeas, rinsed and drained
a small pinch of saffron, 4 to 6 strands
2-inch piece cinnamon stick
1 tablespoon honey
⅔ cup dried apricots
sea salt and freshly ground black pepper
juice of ½ lemon, to serve
1 handful parsley leaves, chopped, to serve
steamed rice, to serve

GOES WELL WITH
Turkish Lentil Soup (see page 14)
Lebanese Lemon and Vanilla Cake (page 198)

Marinated Lamb Chops with a Spicy Mango Salsa

SERVES 4

1½ tablespoons freshly ground black
    pepper
4 garlic cloves
2 lemongrass stalks
½ cup oyster sauce
3 tablespoons light soy sauce
juice of 1 lime
2 tablespoons vegetable oil
8 lamb chops
½ red chili, seeded and finely sliced,
    to serve
1 small handful cilantro leaves,
    to serve

FOR THE SALSA

1 large mango, peeled, pitted and finely
    diced
1 red chili, seeded and finely chopped
a large bunch cilantro leaves, finely
    chopped
juice of 2 limes

GOES WELL WITH

Chinese Tiger Salad (page 26)
Malaysian Spice Garden Shrimp
    Curry (page 138)
Char Kueh Toew (Fried Rice Noodles
    with Shrimp and Egg) (page 193)

1 Put the black pepper and garlic into a mini food processor and blend into a rough paste, then transfer it to a large mixing bowl.

2 Bash the fat ends of the lemongrass stalks a couple of times with a heavy spoon to help release their delicious flavor, and add to the mixing bowl with the pepper and garlic paste. Add the oyster sauce, soy sauce, lime juice and oil to the bowl and mix until well combined. Drop in the lamb chops and mix until they are well coated. Cover the bowl and leave to marinate at room temperature 30 minutes, or overnight in the refrigerator if time allows.

3 Meanwhile, gently mix the salsa ingredients together in a bowl until well combined and set aside.

4 Preheat the oven to 400°F. Put the chops and marinade in a shallow roasting tray and pour the marinade over the top. Bake 12 to 15 minutes until they are brown on the outside but still pink in the middle.

5 Serve with a spoonful of the cooking juices poured over, a scattering of red chili and cilantro leaves and a good dollop of the salsa.

Za'atar Lamb Cutlets

Za'atar is a wonderful Middle Eastern seasoning made from dried herbs, such as thyme, oregano and mint, mixed with sesame seeds and lovely sour sumac. It's delicious with anything from meat and fish to eggplants and flat bread. If you can't get hold of sumac, then substitute the same quantity of lemon zest, which will provide a similarly sharp flavor.

SERVES 4
8 lamb cutlets, trimmed
2 tablespoons olive oil

FOR THE ZAATAR
2 tablespoons dried thyme
1 tablespoon sumac
1 teaspoon sea salt
3 teaspoons sesame seeds

GOES WELL WITH
Fattoush Salad (see page 32)
Sri Lankan Fried Rice with Cashew
    Nuts and Egg (page 182)
Tropical Fruit Salad with a Chili,
    Star Anise, Cinnamon and Lime
    Dressing (page 210)

1 To make the za'atar, put the thyme, sumac, salt and 2 teaspoons of the sesame seeds into a spice grinder and grind to a coarse powder. Transfer to a mixing bowl and add the last teaspoon of sesame seeds.

2 Add the lamb cutlets and oil to the bowl and use your hands to rub the za'atar mix and oil into the lamb, making sure the cutlets are completely covered. Leave to marinate 30 minutes, or overnight in the refrigerator if time allows.

3 Heat a griddle pan, or skillet if you don't have one, over high heat until smoking, then add the lamb cutlets. Cook 3 to 4 minutes on each side, or until the lamb is brown on the outside and beautifully pink and juicy inside. Leave to rest 2 minutes, then serve.

Indian Seekh Kebabs

This recipe works best with ground meat that has quite a bit of fat so everything stays moist. If, however, you want to go lean, no problem —just make sure you turn the kebabs more regularly and reduce the cooking time by a couple of minutes, as leaner meat burns more easily.

1　If using wooden skewers for this recipe, soak them in warm water 30 minutes.

2　Put the lamb, garlic, ginger and green chilies into a food processor and blend 2 minutes, or until the mixture forms a very smooth paste and sticks together in a ball. Transfer to a large mixing bowl and add the egg, cilantro, garam masala, mustard powder and salt and mix really well. Using your fists, punch down on the mixture several times to tenderize the meat—harness some aggression! Pour in the cream, mix, cover and place in the freezer 15 minutes, which makes it easier to shape the kebabs.

3　Meanwhile, preheat the broiler to high. Wet your hands, then take a golf ball-size piece of lamb and push it onto the top of a metal or wooden skewer. Pull the lamb down the skewer, twisting as you go to help stretch the meat over the skewer about 4 inches. Keep the width as even as possible. Repeat with the remaining lamb mixture.

4　Brush each kebab with a little oil and place under the hot broiler 5 or 6 minutes, turning every 2 minutes, until the kebab is golden and cooked through. Serve with yogurt and lemon wedges for squeezing over.

SERVES 4

14 ounces ground lamb leg
4 garlic cloves, finely chopped
2-inch piece gingerroot, peeled and
　finely chopped
2 green chilies, seeded and finely
　chopped
½ beaten egg
1 large handful cilantro leaves, finely
　chopped
1½ teaspoons garam masala
2 teaspoons mustard powder or French
　mustard
1 teaspoon sea salt
¼ cup heavy cream
olive oil, for brushing
plain yogurt, to serve
1 lemon, cut into wedges, to serve

GOES WELL WITH
Charred Eggplants with Indian Spices
　and Cilantro (page 161)
Herb and Spice Pilaf Rice (page 181)

Broiled Lamb Skewers with a Bulgur Wheat Salad

SERVES 4
1 red chili, seeded
4 garlic cloves
2 teaspoons ground cumin
2 teaspoons ground coriander
½ teaspoon ground cinnamon
4 tablespoons olive oil
1¾ pounds boned, trimmed lamb leg,
    cut into 1-inch cubes
sea salt and freshly ground black pepper
plain yogurt, to serve

FOR THE BULGUR WHEAT SALAD
1½ cups bulgur wheat
1 cup roughly chopped sun-dried
    tomatoes
½ red onion, finely chopped
1 red chili, seeded and finely chopped
1 handful dill leaves, finely chopped,
    plus extra sprigs to serve
1 large handful parsley leaves, finely
    chopped
juice of ½ lemon
2 tablespoons olive oil

GOES WELL WITH
Feta, Walnut and Nigella Seed Salad
    (page 21)

1 Put the red chili and garlic in a mini food processor with a good pinch of salt and grind to a smooth paste. Add the cumin, coriander, cinnamon and olive oil and blend until lovely and smooth. Transfer to a large mixing bowl, add the lamb and mix everything together until all the meat is well coated. Cover with plastic wrap and set aside to marinate 30 minutes, or overnight in the refrigerator if time allows.

2 Soak four wooden skewers in water 30 minutes. This will stop them from burning under the broiler later.

3 To make the bulgur wheat salad, cook the bulgar wheat in a saucepan of boiling water 8 to 10 minutes until tender but still with just a little bite. Transfer to a strainer, rinse with cold water and drain, squeezing out any excess water with your hands. Tip into a mixing bowl and add the sun-dried tomatoes, onion, red chili, dill, parsley, lemon juice and oil and season with a really good pinch of salt and pepper. Toss everything together until the all the ingredients are well combined.

4 Preheat the broiler to high. Divide the lamb into 4 equal portions and push onto the four soaked skewers. Broil 3 to 4 minutes on each side until the lamb is brown on the outside and pink and juicy in the middle. Serve hot with the bulgur salad, a dollop of plain yogurt, an extra grind of pepper and a scattering of dill sprigs.

Sticky Szechuan Pork with Sesame Seeds

This recipe is Chinese cooking at it's best—the pork belly is cooked slowly with the spices, so it fully absorbs all their delicious Szechuan flavors, and is then coated in a rich sticky sauce. You can leave the skin of the gingerroot on when preparing this dish. Not only does this make the preparation quicker, but according to a friend of mine, Mr. Hung, in Chengdu, the skin adds a better flavor and is very healthy to eat. Frankly, less peeling can only be a good thing! Just make sure the ginger is fresh and that you give it a good wash before you slice it.

SERVES 4

2 tablespoons vegetable oil
4 dried red chilies, roughly chopped
6 star anise
1 pound 2 ounces boneless pork belly, cut into 1-inch-wide pieces
1-inch piece gingerroot, roughly sliced
1 teaspoon sea salt
1 tablespoon rice vinegar
2 tablespoons sugar
1 tablespoon soy sauce
1 tablespoon sesame seeds

GOES WELL WITH

Szechuan Chicken and Cucumber Salad (page 37)
Char Kueh Toew (Fried Rice Noodles with Shrimp and Egg) (page 193)

1 Heat the oil in a wok over high heat. When smoking hot, chuck in the dried red chilies and star anise and stir-fry 30 seconds, or until fragrant. Add the pork belly, ginger and salt and continue stir-frying 2 to 3 minutes longer until the pork starts to take on a little color.

2 Pour 2 cups hot water over, which should just cover everything, and give it a good stir. Bring to a boil, then cover, reduce the heat to low and simmer 1 hour 30 minutes, or until the pork is cooked through and tender. Remove the pork from the wok with a slotted spoon and set aside. Using a spoon, skim off any excess fat from the surface of the liquid left in the wok.

3 Whisk together the vinegar, sugar, soy sauce and 1 tablespoon water in a small bowl and add to the wok. Turn the heat up to high and cook, stirring continuously, 5 minutes, or until the sauce reduces by half.

4 Return the pork to the wok, add the sesame seeds and stir-fry 2 to 3 minutes until the sauce becomes really thick and sticky and the pork is well coated. Sprinkle the sesame seeds over and serve immediately.

Al Pastor Pork and Pineapple Salad

SERVES 4
4 large boned pork chops
2 tablespoons olive oil
¾ pineapple, peeled, cored and finely
    sliced
2 scallions, finely chopped
1 red chili, seeded and chopped
2 large handfuls cilantro leaves, finely
    chopped
juice of 2 limes, plus extra to serve
sea salt and freshly ground pepper

FOR THE MARINADE
¼ teaspoon smoked paprika
½ teaspoon ground cumin
¼ teaspoon ground cloves
2 garlic cloves
2 tomatoes
¼ pineapple, peeled and cored

GOES WELL WITH:
Bangkok Garlic and Black Pepper
    Chicken (page 72)
Tomato and Coconut Rice
    (page 187)

1   To make the marinade, put all the ingredients into a food processor and blend to
    a smooth paste. Pour the mixture into a large mixing bowl, add the pork chops and
    mix until the meat is well coated. Cover and leave to marinate 1 hour, or overnight
    in the refrigerator if time allows.
2   Remove the pork from the mixing bowl, reserving the marinade. Heat the oil
    in a large skillet over medium heat, then add the pork chops and fry on one side
    5 to 6 minutes until golden, then flip them over and pour in half the marinade.
    Cook 5 to 6 minutes longer until the pork is colored and cooked through but still
    lovely and juicy. Remove the pan from the heat and leave to rest 5 minutes.
3   Meanwhile, put the pineapple, scallions, red chili, cilantro and lime juice in a large
    serving bowl and season with a really good pinch of salt and pepper. Mix well
    so everything is coated in the lime juice.
4   Place the pork chops on top of the fresh salad and serve immediately, spooning some
    of the pan juices over the top. Add an extra squeeze of lime to make the pork taste
    even more zesty and delicious.

Twice-Cooked Pork

You'll find this dish on any decent Szechuan menu. The traditional recipe requires chili bean paste, a classic Szechuan flavoring made from chilies and fermented fava beans, but it can be difficult to get hold of so I've come up with an alternative chili paste that works really well. If you like your food really hot, then add an extra half teaspoon of chili flakes to the paste.

1 Bring a large saucepan of water to a boil. Add the pork, turn the heat down to low and simmer 25 minutes, or until the meat is 80 percent cooked through but still pink in the middle. This will prevent the pork from overcooking later. Remove the pork from the water, slice into thin strips and set aside.

2 Meanwhile, put all the chili paste ingredients into a mini food processor and blend until smooth. Pour into a small skillet over high heat with ¼ cup hot water. Bring to a slow boil, reduce the heat and simmer, stirring occasionally, 10 minutes, or until the sauce reduces by about half.

3 Heat a large wok over high heat and add the oil. Once the oil is smoking hot, add the red pepper and stir-fry 30 seconds, then add the pork and stir-fry 5 minutes, or until it is cooked through and tender and starting to take on a lovely color. Finally add the chili sauce, stir-fry 30 seconds and serve immediately.

SERVES 4
1 pound 2 ounces boneless pork leg
1 tablespoon vegetable oil
1 red bell pepper, seeded and roughly
  chopped

FOR THE CHILI PASTE
4 garlic cloves, roughly chopped
1 large mild red chili, seeded and
  roughly chopped
½ teaspoon chili flakes
2½ tablespoons light soy sauce
1 tablespoon vegetable oil
a pinch of sugar

GOES WELL WITH
Crispy Szechuan Tofu (page 167)
Szechuan Noodles with Lamb and
  Peanuts (page 190)

Guyi Cumin, Chili and Soy Ribs

SERVES 4
8 to 12 pork spareibs
olive oil, for brushing

FOR THE SAUCE
3 tablespoons vegetable oil
2 teaspoons cumin seeds
1 teaspoon chili flakes
4 garlic cloves, finely chopped
6 scallions, finely chopped
4 tablespoons soy sauce
1 tablespoon honey

GOES WELL WITH
Jetalah Pineapple, Cucumber and
    Chili Salad (page 30)
Dark Chocolate, Clove and Cinnamon
    Brownies (page 196)

1 Bring a large saucepan of water to a boil, then add the spareribs. Turn the heat down and simmer 45 minutes, or until the meat is tender and cooked through. Drain the ribs in a colander and leave to dry a couple of minutes.

2 Meanwhile, make the sauce. Heat the oil in a small saucepan over medium heat and chuck in the cumin seeds and chili flakes. Leave them to crackle 30 seconds, or until fragrant, then add 3 of the garlic cloves and 5 of the scallions and stir-fry 2 minutes. Pour in the soy sauce, honey and ⅔ cup hot water. Bring to a boil and cook, stirring occasionally, 4 to 5 minutes until the sauce reduces and become sticky.

3 Preheat the broiler to high. Brush the ribs with the sauce and place them under the broiler 3 to 4 minutes on each side until golden. Be sure to brush with more sauce when you turn them over.

4 Place the ribs on a large platter and serve with any leftover sauce on the side, or smother the ribs with sauce, if liked. Sprinkle with the remaining garlic and scallion and serve immediately.

CHAPTER FOUR

Fish and Seafood

Spice are used throughout the world to add a massive sensory hit to so many different fish and seafood dishes. In this chapter I will show you how cooking fish with spices can be really easy. By combining just two spices, earthy yellow turmeric and fragrant lemongrass, for example, you can create all the background flavor needed to make Coconut and Lemongrass Salmon Curry, one of the most delicious curries around. It also shows perfectly that you should never be afraid of cooking with spices. You simply don't need loads of them—just the right ones to bring your food to life. One of my favorite spices is smoked paprika. It's madly burned red in color and brings a delicious sprinkling of barbecue flavors to dishes. With a small amount of this magic spice and some garlic, you get all the rich, smoky flavors of Mexico in the delicious Fish Tacos with a Smoky Paprika and Tomato Salsa.

LEFT: Broiled Thai Sea Bass with Chili, Mint and Roasted Peanuts (page 134)

Meen Molee South Indian Fish Curry

My lovely friend Rosamma showed me how to make this delicious curry at her beautiful home, surrounded by pineapple plants and nutmeg trees, in Kerala. This is a classic example of the fresh, simple food they eat in that region of India but, if you want to jazz it up a bit, you can add a mixture of seafood to the lovely sauce.

SERVES 4

1-inch piece gingerroot, peeled
4 garlic cloves
1 tablespoon vegetable oil
1 large onion, roughly chopped
½ teaspoon mild chili powder
½ teaspoon turmeric
1 large tomato, finely chopped
2 cups coconut cream
juice of 1 lime
1 pound 2 ounces thick white fish fillets,
    such as halibut, haddock, pollack
    or cod, skinned and cut into bite-size
    pieces
sea salt
rice, to serve

GOES WELL WITH

Tamarind and Lemongrass Chicken
    Stir-Fry (page 59)
Gobi Masala (Indian Stir-Fried
    Cauliflower) (page 172)

1 Put the ginger and garlic into a mini food processor and blend to a smooth paste.
2 Heat the oil in a large saucepan over medium heat, then add the onion and fry 2 to 3 minutes until translucent. Add the ginger and garlic paste, chili powder, turmeric and tomatoes and cook 30 seconds, stirring continuously.
3 Add the coconut cream and lime juice and season with a good pinch of salt. Mix well, bring to a boil and add the fish. Reduce the heat to low and simmer 8 to 10 minutes until the fish is opaque and cooked through. Serve immediately with rice.

Sri Lankan Deviled Monkfish

My version of Sri Lankan Deviled Monkfish combines the expert spicing of South Indian cuisine and the umami flavors of Chinese cuisine into a salty, spicy, savory sauce that explodes in your mouth. For this recipe I have used black pepper, dried curry leaves, garlic and gingerroot. The black pepper and chili work together to provide different layers of heat and the curry leaves add all the magnificent flavors of Kerala to contrast with the very Chinese oyster sauce. The garlic and ginger help to pull everything together to give an incredibly delicious eating experience.

1 Place the fish fillets in a large skillet over medium heat and pour in about ½ inch hot water. Cover and bring to a slow boil, then reduce the heat to low and simmer the fish 10 to 12 minutes until the flesh just turns opaque. Remove the pan from the heat and set the fish aside on a plate, reserving the cooking liquid.

2 Meanwhile, heat a wok over high heat and add the oil. When the oil is hot, throw in the garlic and ginger and stir-fry 10 seconds, or until fragrant. Add the onion, tomatoes, black pepper and a pinch of salt, then stir-fry 2 to 3 minutes until the onions are starting to soften.

3 Rub the dried curry leaves between your hands so they break up and scatter them over the top of the tomato mixture. Add the oyster sauce and 4 tablespoons of the fish cooking liquid and mix well. Pour the sauce over the fish and serve immediately.

SERVES 4

4 monkfish fillets, about 7 ounces each, skinned
2 tablespoons vegetable oil
2 garlic cloves, thinly sliced
1-inch piece gingerroot, peeled and thinly sliced
1 red onion, thinly sliced
2 tomatoes, finely chopped
½ teaspoon freshly ground black pepper
a large pinch dried curry leaves
2 tablespoons oyster sauce
sea salt

GOES WELL WITH

Coconut and Chili Kerabu Salad
(page 29)
Sri Lankan Fried Rice with Cashew
Nuts and Egg (page 182)

Cha Ca La Vong

Vietnamese Turmeric- and Chili-Spiced Cod with Rice Noodles, Peanuts and Herbs

Cha Ca La Vong is a famous restaurant in Hanoi that serves just one dish: "Cha Ca," or fried fish. It is served at your table with scallions in a frying pan, sizzling, on top of a small barbecue.

SERVES 4

⅓ cup unsalted peanuts, chopped
9 ounces rice noodles
6 tablespoons vegetable oil
1 handful dill, chopped
1 handful cilantro leaves, chopped
1 handful mint leaves, chopped
1 tablespoon turmeric
4 tablespoons all-purpose flour
4 cod fillets, about 7 ounces each,
    skinned and cut into bite-size pieces
8 to 10 scallions, halved and thinly
    sliced lengthwise
2 tablespoons fish sauce
juice of ½ lime
½ red chili, seeded and finely chopped

GOES WELL WITH

Mango, Orange and Nutmeg
    Cheesecake (page 204)

1 Heat a skillet over medium heat. Add the peanuts and gently toast, shaking the pan occasionally, 2 to 3 minutes until the peanuts are a beautiful golden brown. Transfer the nuts to a plate to cool.

2 Cook the noodles according to the package directions, then drain and immediately refresh under cold water. Drain well. Transfer to a bowl, dress with 2 tablespoons of the oil to stop them sticking and set aside. Put the dill, cilantro and mint together into one bowl and the peanuts into another.

3 In a large mixing bowl, mix together the turmeric and flour. Dip the cod pieces into the flour, making sure every piece is completely coated.

4 Heat the remaining oil in a large skillet over medium heat and fry the cod, turning occasionally, 2 to 3 minutes until the flesh turns opaque and is flaky to the touch.

5 Add the scallions, fish sauce and lime juice and gently mix until well combined.

6 Scatter the red chili over the top and serve with the noodles, herbs and peanuts on the side to mix together as you like.

Turmeric

Also called "Indian saffron," turmeric is a very old spice native to India, which is still the major producer of the spice today. It was first cultivated around 3,000 B.C. by the Harappan civilization in the Indus Valley. The beautiful spice was used in cosmetics, cooking, medicine and as a dye, which all still remains the case today. The wonderful root has been praised in Ayurvedic medicine for centuries as an important anti-inflammatory, antioxident and vital aid to digestion. And as I discovered during my recent travels to India, often when turmeric is added to a curry, "for health" is pronounced.

Turmeric is part of the ginger family, and if I am going to get technical, like ginger, it is a rhizome: a horizontal mass of the stem of a plant that is found growing underground. The best thing about turmeric, however, is its madly orange color. If you are ever lucky enough to get hold of the fresh "root," you're in for a treat. The muddy yellow-colored root, when broken open, reveals an intensely deep, bright orange colored root. It's so amazing! In Southeast Asia the root is often used fresh, either grated or simply cut up and pickled. The flavor is very distinct—earthy and slightly bitter—and it provides the color of a beautiful, deep orange evening sunshine to curries, stir-frys and curry powders. To make the yellow turmeric powder we all know, the root is boiled, dried and ground.

Due to the intensity of color and flavor, turmeric should be used sparingly. I tend to buy it in small amounts, which can be kept for up to six months. To keep its flavor, store this golden spice in a dry, airtight container out of direct sunlight. If you are using turmeric in a spice rub, I strongly recommend putting on a pair of rubber gloves before you start.

Indian Fish Cakes with a Cilantro and Coconut Chutney

SERVES 4
14 ounces salmon fillets, skinned
2 large handfuls cilantro leaves, roughly chopped
1 green chili, seeded and roughly chopped
1 teaspoon garam masala
1 teaspoon ground coriander
½ teaspoon sea salt
2 tablespoons vegetable oil

FOR THE CHUTNEY
1 handful cilantro leaves
1 handful mint leaves
¼ teaspoon garam masala
juice of ½ lemon
scant ½ cup coconut milk
a pinch of sea salt

GOES WELL WITH
Shrimp and Lemongrass Rice Noodle Salad (page 46)
Roasted Cambodian Eggplants with Ginger and Coconut (page 170)
Herb and Spice Pilaf Rice (page 180)

1   To make the chutney, put all the ingredients into a food processor and blend into a smooth paste. Tip into a bowl and set aside.

2   Put the salmon, cilantro, green chili, garam masala, coriander and salt into the food processor and pulse until everything just binds together in a rough paste. Tip into a large mixing bowl, cover with plastic wrap and chill in the refrigerator about 30 minutes.

3   Divide the mixture up into 4 equal portions. Shape each one into a ball and then flatten on a clean cutting board with the palm of your hand.

4   Heat the oil in a large skillet over medium heat, then gently fry the fish cakes 3 to 4 minutes on each side until golden and crispy. Serve immediately with loads of the delicious chutney.

Creamy Cilantro Swordfish with a Red Onion Raita

1 To make the raita, mix all the ingredients in a large mixing bowl. Season well with salt and pepper, then set aside while you prepare the swordfish, so all the fresh flavors develop.

2 Heat 2 tablespoons of the oil in a large skillet over medium heat. Fry the swordfish fillets 3 to 4 minutes on each side until milky white and flaky to the touch. Remove from the pan and set aside.

3 Heat the remaining 2 tablespoons oil in a large saucepan over medium heat, then scatter in the green chili and garlic and stir-fry 1 to 2 minutes until the garlic starts to turn golden. Add the coriander, black pepper and a good pinch of salt and cook 10 seconds until fragrant. Add the cilantro and 7 tablespoons freshly boiled water. Bring to a boil, then turn the heat down to low and simmer, stirring occasionally, 8 to 10 minutes until the cilantro starts to wilt but is still a vivid green color. Pour in the heavy cream and lemon juice and stir until the liquid forms a creamy sauce.

4 Flake the swordfish fillets into the sauce. Gently mix until the fish is completely coated, then simmer 1 minute, or until the swordfish is heated through. Serve immediately with the raita.

SERVES 4

4 tablespoons olive oil
4 swordfish fillets, about 7 ounces each, skinned
2 green chilies, seeded and finely chopped
4 garlic cloves, thinly sliced
2 teaspoons ground coriander
½ teaspoon freshly ground black pepper
4 handfuls cilantro leaves, finely chopped
⅔ cup heavy cream
juice of 1 lemon
sea salt and freshly ground black pepper

FOR THE RAITA

½ cucumber, seeded and thinly sliced
1 red onion, thinly sliced
½ cup plain yogurt
1 teaspoon ground coriander
juice of 1 lemon

GOES WELL WITH

Feta, Walnut and Nigella Seed Salad (page 21)
Lebanese Lemon and Vanilla Cake (page 198)

Sea Bass Ceviche

Ceviche is a delicious, refreshing dish served all along the coast of Mexico and South America. The fish "cooks" in the lime juice, without using any heat, so you really have to use the freshest fish you can buy. Don't use anything that's been frozen.

1 Spread the sea bass slices out in a shallow dish, add the lime juice and season with a really good pinch of salt. Turn the pieces over, and continue turning them, until the fish is completely coated. Leave to marinate, stirring occasionally, 15 to 20 minutes until the flesh kturns opaque.
2 Meanwhile, cut the tomatoes in half, squeeze out the seeds and finely chop the flesh. This is so the ceviche isn't watery.
3 Put the marinated fish and all its juices in a large mixing bowl with the tomatoes, red chili, cilantro, onion, romaine lettuce, oil and a really good pinch of pepper. Gently mix together and serve immediately.

SERVES 4

9 ounces very fresh firm sea bass fillets, skinned and very thinly sliced
juice of 4 limes
2 tomatoes
1 red chili, seeded and finely chopped
2 large handfuls cilantro leaves, roughly chopped
1 red onion, finely chopped
½ small romaine lettuce, thinly sliced
2 tablespoons olive oil
sea salt and freshly ground black pepper

GOES WELL WITH

Coconut and Chili Kerabu Salad
(page 29)
Shrimp and Lemongrass Rice Noodle
Salad (page 46)
Steamed Ginger Custard Pots
(page 199)

Steamed Cod in a Banana Leaf

This is another wonderfully tasty dish from South India. Frying the fish in a banana leaf adds a really lovely smoky flavor and keeps in all of the delicious juices. You can find banana leaves online or in specialist food stores, but if you don't want to go to the trouble, use baking parchment instead—the recipes will work just as well. You can make everything well in advance and just cook the packages just before serving.

SERVES 4
6 tablespoons vegetable oil
2 teaspoons mustard seeds
4 red onions, finely chopped
2 large pinches of dried curry leaves
2 teaspoons garam masala
juice of 1 lemon
4 large squares banana leaf or baking
    parchment, about 12 x 12 inches
    each
4 cod fillets, about 5 ounces each,
    skinned
4 fresh curry leaves
sea salt

GOES WELL WITH
Sri Lankan Fried Potatoes
    (page 166)
Roasted Cambodian Eggplants with
    Ginger and Coconut (page 170)
Vanilla and Honey Syllabub
    (page 202)

1 Heat 4 tablespoons of the oil in a skillet over medium-low heat, then chuck in the mustard seeds. Let them crackle 30 seconds, then add the onions and cook, stirring occasionally, 10 to 12 minutes until they are really golden and sticky. Rub the dried curry leaves between your hands so they break up, then scatter them over the onions. Add the garam masala and lemon juice and season with a good pinch of salt. Mix well and cook 1 minute longer.

2 Spoon a heaped tablespoon of the cooked onion mixture onto the middle of a banana leaf, then use the back of the spoon to spread the onion so it's just wide enough for one of the fish fillets to sit on top. Place the cod fillets on top of the onion mixture, then spread another heaped spoonful of the onion mixture over and top with a curry leaf. Wrap the fish in the banana leaf like a package, tucking in the sides, and fasten the top with a wooden toothpick. Repeat with the remaining pieces of fish.

3 Add the remaining 2 tablespoons of oil to any remaining onion mixture in the skillet and heat over medium-low heat. Add the fish packages and cook 16 to 18 minutes until the fish is cooked through and tender.

4 Serve immediately, still wrapped in the banana leaf so there is no risk of losing any of the delicious juices.

Black Pepper- and Chili-Seared Tuna with a Carrot and Apple Salad

SERVES 4
4 garlic cloves
1 teaspoon coarsely ground black
  pepper
1 teaspoon chili flakes
4 tablespoons olive oil
1 teaspoon sea salt
¼ teaspoon sugar
4 tuna steaks, about 5 ounces each

FOR THE SALAD
⅓ cup unsalted peanuts
2 tomatoes, seeded and thinly sliced
2 apples, quartered, cored, thinly sliced
  and drizzled in lime juice to stop
  them discoloring
4 large carrots, peeled and grated
3 scallions, thinly sliced
2 red chilies, seeded and thinly sliced
1 handful mint leaves, finely chopped
1 large handful cilantro leaves, roughly
  chopped

FOR THE DRESSING
juice of 2 limes
1 tablespoon fish sauce
1 tablespoon sugar

GOES WELL WITH
Cardamom and Pistachio Nut Kulfi
  (page 205)

1 Heat a skillet over medium heat. Add the peanuts and gently toast, shaking the pan occasionally, 2 to 3 minutes until the peanuts are a beautiful golden brown. Transfer the nuts to a plate to cool.

2 Put the garlic in a mini food processor and blend to a smooth paste. Tip in the black pepper, chili flakes, 2 tablespoons of the oil, the salt and sugar and blend a coarse paste. Rub the paste all over the tuna steaks and leave to marinate 10 minutes. Rinse the mini food processor.

3 Whisk the dressing ingredients together in a large mixing bowl. Give the toasted peanuts a quick blast in a mini food processor until coarsely ground, then add to the mixing bowl along with the other salad ingredients. Toss together so the wonderfully sour Thai flavors in the dressing coat everything.

4 Heat a large griddle pan over medium heat and add the remaining 2 tablespoons oil. Fry the tuna steaks 1 to 2 minutes on each side, or until changing color. Remove the griddle pan from the heat but leave the tuna in the pan 1 to 2 minutes longer. This makes sure the tuna is beautifully seared on the outside but still pink in the middle.

5 Divide the salad into four serving bowls. Slice each tuna steak into 4 pieces and place on top of each salad. Serve immediately.

Broiled Red Snapper with a Mexican Salsa Verde and Corn Salad

1 To make the salsa verde, put all the ingredients into a food processor with a scant ½ cup water and blend until smooth.

2 Preheat the broiler to high. Brush a little oil over each piece of fish and season with salt and pepper. Place under the hot broiler, skin side up, and broil 2 to 3 minutes on each side until just tender and flaky.

3 Meanwhile, in a mixing bowl, toss together the cherry tomatoes, corn, mint, lime juice and oil and season with a good pinch of salt and pepper. Serve immediately with the broiled fish and vibrant salsa.

SERVES 4
2 tablespoons olive oil, plus extra for brushing
4 red snapper fillets, skin on, about 4 ounces each
1½ cups halves cherry tomatoes
1 cup corn kernels
1 small handful mint leaves, finely chopped
juice of 1 lime
sea salt and freshly ground black pepper

FOR THE MEXICAN SALSA VERDE
1 garlic clove
1 green jalapeño chili
6 scallions
1 tomato
2 large handfuls cilantro leaves
2 large handfuls mint leaves
2 large handfuls parsley leaves
juice of 3 limes
2 tablespoons olive oil
sea salt and freshly ground black pepper

GOES WELL WITH
Nasi Goreng (Indonesian Fried Rice) (page 186)
Cambodian Caramelized Ginger Bananas with Vanilla Ice Cream (page 212)

Fish Tacos with a Smoky Paprika and Tomato Salsa

1 To make the salsa, heat a skillet over high heat until smoking hot. Add the tomatoes, garlic and onion and char on all sides 5 to 6 minutes until they are blackened and tender. Remove the skillet from the heat. Once cool enough to handle, skin the onion and garlic. Put the tomatoes, garlic, onion, paprika, lime juice, oil and honey into a food processor, season with a good pinch of salt and pepper and blend until lovely and smooth. Pour the salsa back into the skillet over medium heat, bring to a slow boil, then reduce the heat to low and simmer, stirring occasionally, 15 minutes. This lets all the flavors develop.

2 Heat 2 tablespoons of the oil in a large skillet over medium heat and add the fish, skin side down. Cook 2 minutes, then flip the fillets over, turn off the heat and leave 2 minutes longer to finish cooking.

3 Meanwhile, heat the remaining tablespoon of oil in a small skillet over medium heat and add the prosciutto, if using. Fry really quickly, just 10 to 20 seconds, until the ham is lovely and crisp. Stir continuously so it doesn't burn.

4 Flake the fish into a large mixing bowl with the salsa, prosciutto, mozzarella, cherry tomatoes, scallions and romaine lettuce. Toss everything together and divide onto the the four tortillas. Roll each into a cone shape and serve.

SERVES 4

3 tablespoons olive oil
4 sea bass fillets, skin on, about
   4 ounces each
4 slices prosciutto (optional)
1 cup finely chopped mozzarella
8 cherry tomatoes, finely chopped
4 scallions, finely chopped
1 romaine lettuce, finely chopped
4 corn tortillas

FOR THE SALSA

2 tomatoes
2 garlic cloves, unpeeled
1 red onion, unpeeled and cut in half
½ teaspoon smoked paprika
juice of ½ lime
2 tablespoons olive oil
½ tablespoon honey
sea salt and freshly ground black pepper

GOES WELL WITH

Guacamole and Shrimp Salad
   (page 42)
Mexican Cinnamon Peaches
   (page 206)

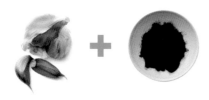

Broiled Thai Sea Bass with Chili, Mint and Roasted Peanuts

SERVES 4
⅓ cup unsalted peanuts
4 whole sea bass, 10 to 12 ounces each,
    dressed and trimmed
olive oil, for brushing
juice of 1 lime
1 tablespoon fish sauce
1 teaspoon sugar
1 red chili, seeded and thinly sliced
    lengthwise
1 cucumber, seeded and thinly sliced
1 red onion, thinly sliced
2 large handfuls mint leaves
sea salt and fresh ground black pepper

GOES WELL WITH
Nasi Goreng (Indonesian Fried Rice)
    (page 186)
Margarita on the Rocks with a
    Chili Rim (page 215)

1 Heat a skillet over medium heat. Add the peanuts and gently toast, shaking the
   pan occasionally, 2 to 3 minutes, or until the peanuts are a beautiful golden brown.
   Transfer the nuts to a plate to cool, then roughly chop.

2 Preheat the broiler to medium. With a sharp knife, make a few diagonal slashes on
   each side of the sea bass, then brush each fish lightly with oil and season with
   a pinch of salt and pepper. Place the fish under the broiler 5 to 7 minutes on each
   side, or until the skin is crisp and the flesh cooked through.

3 Meanwhile, whisk the lime juice, fish sauce and sugar together in a bowl, then stir
   in the red chili, cucumber and onion.

4 Divide the sea bass onto four plates and spoon the chili sauce over. Scatter the
   toasted and chopped peanuts and mint on top and serve immediately.

Coconut and Lemongrass Salmon Curry

What I love about this delicious curry is there are only two, highly complementary spices involved—turmeric and lemongrass. The turmeric gives the curry a sunshine-yellow color and a deep, earthy taste, while the lemongrass freshens up the sauce with its citrus fragrance. The classic Southeast Asian salty and sour flavors, which come from the fish sauce and lime juice, cut through the rich coconut and bring the dish to life. This is a perfect example of how you can create an exotic curry with only a few simple spices.

1 Heat a large saucepan over medium heat and add the oil. When hot, add the onion and cook, stirring occasionally, for 5 to 6 minutes until soft.

2 Bash the fat ends of the lemongrass stalks a couple of times with a heavy spoon to help release their delicious flavor. Add them to the saucepan along with the turmeric and cook 30 seconds, stirring continuously, then pour the coconut cream, lime juice, fish sauce and sugar over and mix well. Bring to a boil, then cover, reduce the heat to low and simmer 10 minutes, stirring occasionally.

3 Add the salmon pieces, then cook, uncovered, 8 to 10 minutes longer until the fish is tender and the sauce is lovely and thick. Throw in the cilantro, gently mix together and serve immediately with rice.

SERVES 4
2 tablespoons vegetable oil
1 onion, finely chopped
2 lemongrass stalks
¼ teaspoon turmeric
2 cups coconut cream
juice of 1 lime
1 tablespoon fish sauce
a pinch of sugar
1 pound 2 ounces salmon fillets,
    skinned and cut into bite-size pieces
1 large handful cilantro leaves, roughly
    chopped
rice, to serve

GOES WELL WITH
Jetalah Pineapple, Cucumber and
    Chili Salad (page 30)
Sri Lankan Fried Potatoes
    (page 166)
Sri Lankan Fried Rice with Cashew
    Nuts and Egg (page 182)

Alleppy Shrimp Curry

SERVES 4
2 tablespoons vegetable oil
2 teaspoons mustard seeds
2 cups coconut cream
juice of 1 lemon
1 pound 2 ounces raw jumbo shrimp,
    shelled and deveined
a large pinch of dried curry leaves
rice, to serve

FOR THE CURRY PASTE
1 green chili, seeded
1 red onion, roughly chopped
2-inch piece gingerroot, peeled and
    roughly chopped
½ teaspoon turmeric
sea salt

GOES WELL WITH
Szechuann Noodles with Lamb and
    Peanuts (page 190)
Char Kueh Toew (Fried Rice Noodles
    with Shrimp and Egg) (page 193)

1 To make the curry paste, put all the ingredients into a mini food processor, season with a good pinch of salt and grind to a smooth paste.

2 Heat the oil in a large skillet over medium heat, then throw in the mustard seeds. When they start popping after about 30 seconds, add the curry paste and stir-fry 30 seconds longer until fragrant.

3 Pour in the coconut cream and lemon juice and bring to a boil. Reduce the heat to low and simmer, stirring occasionally, 10 minutes, or until the sauce reduces and is really thick.

4 Add the shrimp and simmer, stirring frequently so they cook evenly, 5 minutes, or until they turn pink and cook through. Rub the dried curry leaves between your hands so they break up and scatter over the curry. Mix well and serve immediately with rice.

Malaysian Spice Garden Shrimp Curry

SERVES 4
2 tablespoons vegetable oil
1¾ cups coconut milk
juice of ½ lime
1 pound 2 ounces raw jumbo shrimp,
    shelled and deveined
sea salt

FOR THE CURRY PASTE
2 lemongrass stalks
1 red chili, seeded and roughly chopped
2 garlic cloves
1-inch piece gingerroot, roughly
    chopped
½ teaspoon turmeric
¼ teaspoon shrimp paste

GOES WELL WITH
Coconut and Chili Kerabu Salad
    (page 29)
Tomato and Coconut Rice
    (page 187)

1 To prepare the curry paste, remove the really tough outer leaves of the lemongrass and cut off the ends of the stalks. Starting at the fatter end, roughly slice each lemongrass stalk into rings. You should see a purple band in the rings. Stop slicing when there are no more purple bands, as the tops will be too tough to eat. Set the tops aside to add to the curry later and put the sliced lemongrass in a mini food processor. Add the other curry paste ingredients and blend to a smooth paste.

2 Heat the oil in a large saucepan over medium heat. Add the curry paste and stir-fry 30 seconds, or until fragrant.

3 Add the coconut milk, lime juice and reserved tops of the lemongrass stalks and season with a pinch of salt. Mix well and bring to a boil, then reduce the heat to low. Add the shrimp and simmer 5 minutes, or until they turn pink and are cooked through. Remove the lemongrass tops and serve immediately.

Shrimp with Ginger and Chili

1 Heat a wok over high heat and add the oil. When hot, add the onion, ginger and green chili and stir-fry for 2–3 minutes, or until the onion starts to turn golden.

2 Rub the curry leaves between your hands so that they break up and scatter them over the onion. Add the shrimp, turmeric, lemon juice and 2 tablespoons water and season with a pinch of salt. Continue to stir-fry for 2–3 minutes, or until the shrimp have turned pink and are cooked through. Serve immediately.

SERVES 4

2 tablespoons vegetable oil
1 red onion, thinly sliced
1-inch piece gingerroot, peeled and thinly sliced into matchsticks
1 green chili, seeded and thinly sliced
a large pinch of dried curry leaves
1 pound 2 ounces raw jumbo shrimp, peeled and deveined
½ teaspoon turmeric
juice of ½ lemon
sea salt

GOES WELL WITH

Vietnamese Star Anise and Lemongrass Chicken Claypot (page 61)
Red Lentil Dal (page 174)
Mango, Orange and Nutmeg Cheesecake (page 201)

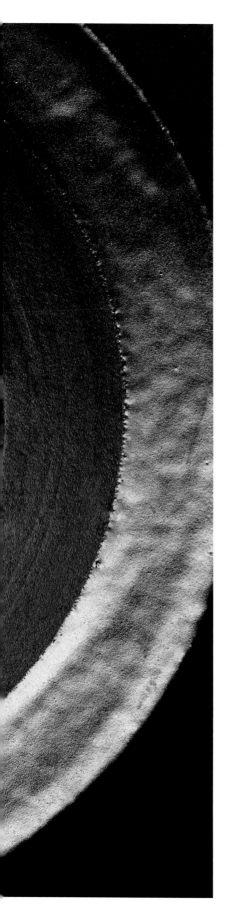

Ginger

Ginger is a wonderful, bulbous root that has a brilliant fresh, slightly peppery, fragrant taste and a sweet juicy smell. For centuries ginger has been used for its culinary and medicinal purposes. It was first mentioned in the 5th century B.C. by the Chinese philosopher Confucius, and the name is derived from the ancient Sanskrit word *stringa-vera*, which means "with a body like a horn." Today it has a huge variety of culinary uses and is still regarded as a fantastic aid for digestion and an alternative cure for nausea.

In the East, ginger is commonly used for savory dishes, while in the West, in sweet dishes. It comes in a variety of different forms: fresh (my favorite), pickled, powdered, preserved or crystallized, and each different form has very different uses.

When you buy a piece of fresh gingerroot, you want to look for a really fat, juicy bit, with a thin, light brown skin that will rub off really easily if you scratch a small area with your fingernail. If the skin doesn't rub of easily, and the ginger looks tired and saggy, it will have lost its moisture and freshness and won't taste great.

Ginger is really fibrous, so large bits can be tough and stringy to eat. To prepare your ginger, remove the skin with a small, sharp knife and cut the root into small sections you can then thinly slice into thin matchsticks, finely chop or grate, which removes the fibrous part and is ideal for salad dressings. You can also grind the finely chopped ginger into a paste using a mini food processor, spice grinder or mortar and pestle.

Malay Yellow Mussel Curry

SERVES 4
2 tablespoons vegetable oil
1¾ cups coconut milk
juice of ½ lemon
2¼ pounds mussels, cleaned and beards removed
1 large handful cilantro leaves

FOR THE CURRY PASTE
2 lemongrass stalks
1-inch piece gingerroot, peeled
2 garlic cloves
⅓ cup unsalted cashew nuts
½ teaspoon shrimp paste
½ teaspoon chili flakes
½ teaspoon turmeric

GOES WELL WITH
Indian Chicken, Pomegranate and
    Herb Salad (page 38)
Char Kueh Toew (Fried Rice Noodles
    with Shrimp and Egg) (page 193)

1 To prepare the curry paste, remove the really tough outer leaves from the lemongrass and cut off the ends of the stalks. Starting at the fatter end, roughly slice each lemongrass stalk into rings. You should see a purple band in the rings. Stop slicing when there are no more purple bands and discard the rest of the lemongrass, as it will be too tough to eat. Put the lemongrass slices in a mini food processor with the other curry paste ingredients and blend to a smooth paste.

2 Heat the oil in a large wok over medium heat. Add the curry paste and stir-fry 30 seconds, or until fragrant, then pour in the coconut milk and lemon juice. Mix well and bring to a boil, then turn the heat down to low and simmer, stirring occasionally, 5 minutes.

3 Discard any open mussels that do not snap shut when tapped. Carefully add the mussels to the coconut mixture, then cover and cook, shaking the pan occasionally, 5 to 6 minutes until nearly all the mussel shells are open.

4 Remove the mussels from the heat and divide them into four bowls, discarding any mussles that are still closed. Scatter the cilantro over and serve immediately.

Stir-Fried Squid with Chili and Cilantro

My first night in Bangkok during my travels was a disaster. Despite not having been there for ten years, I thought I knew the city like the back of my hand. I wandered around, and much to my disappointment, ate nothing of any merit, so the next day I took no chances and stuck to what I know best —food markets. I went to Tor Kor market, in the north of the city, which was full of hungry office workers looking for lunch. Forget a cheeky chicken and bacon sandwich, this place had amazing curries and noodles, braised pork with green beans, clams in a red curry sauce, grilled satay, oyster omelets, papaya salads—and this brilliantly hot, stir-fried squid. If I could have this dish as a quick working lunch every day, I would be a very happy man.

1 Cut the squid tentacles from the squid tube and keep whole, then cut open the tubes and, using a sharp knife, score in a crisscross pattern on the inside.
2 Heat the oil in a wok over medium heat. When hot, add the chili flakes and garlic, stir-fry 30 seconds, or until fragrant and then add the squid. Stir-fry 2 to 3 minutes longer until the squid is pale and cooked through. Pour the oyster sauce, fish sauce and lime juice over and continue stir-frying 30 seconds to combine.
3 Throw in the cilantro, mix well and serve immediately.

SERVES 4
1 pound 9 ounces baby squid, dressed
2 tablespoons vegetable oil
1 teaspoon chili flakes
2 garlic cloves, finely chopped
2 tablespoons oyster sauce
1 tablespoon fish sauce
juice of ½ lime
1 large handful cilantro leaves, roughly chopped

GOES WELL WITH
Stir-Fried Beef with Black Pepper and Basil (page 89)
Nasi Goreng (Indonesian Fried Rice) (page 186)

Chili and Basil Scallops

For many years my brother Tom has been a loyal eating companion of mine, a wingman, who loves his food and is also real fun to go out with. Annoyingly he's moved to Hong Kong with his lovely wife Rachel to live, which makes dinner a bit more difficult to organize. Tom's first choice whenever we do get to go out is something with scallops, so these beautiful, Asian-inspired scallops are here to keep him happy. Now all he has to do is cook them for me.

SERVES 4
2 tablespoons vegetable oil
4 garlic cloves, finely chopped
2 red chilies, seeded and finely chopped
1 red onion, thinly sliced
1 pound 2 ounces scallops, with
  or without roe attached
1 tablespoon light soy sauce
1 tablespoon fish sauce
¼ teaspoon sugar
½ teaspoon coarsely ground black
  pepper
2 large handfuls basil leaves, roughly
  chopped

GOES WELL WITH
Gung Bao Chicken (page 60)
Beijing Teahouse Vegetable Stir-Fry
  (page 169)

1 Heat the oil in a large wok over high heat. When smoking hot, chuck in the garlic and red chilies and stir-fry 30 seconds, or until fragrant. Add the onion and stir-fry 1 minute, then tip in the scallops and stir-fry 1 to 2 minutes longer, or until the scallops start to turn golden at the edges.

2 Pour in the soy sauce and fish sauce and sprinkle in the sugar and black pepper. Mix well and stir-fry 1 minute, or until the scallops are just cooked through and tender. Throw in the basil leaves, mix well and serve immediately. You can use scallop shells for presentation, if you like.

CHAPTER FIVE

Vegetarian

Vegetarian food should be exciting and versatile, and in this chapter I will show you how—with five spices or less—you can create some really superb dishes. Delicious falafel, Mexican eggs with a wonderful kick, quesadillas with a brilliantly green dipping sauce flavored with chili; garlic and cumin; a Lebanese pizza; curries; stir-frys; dal; zingy refried beans; and the most amazing eggplant recipe are all here. There are loads of delicious ways to cook eggplants, but Charred Eggplants with Indian Spices and Cilantro, which only uses four spices—fresh green chili, garam masala, turmeric and ground coriander—is up there as one of the most spectacular you'll ever eat.

LEFT: Cambodian Street-Style Vegetable Curry (page 160)

Falafel Burgers with a Yogurt and Tahini Dip

SERVES 4
½ red onion, roughly chopped
½ green chili, seeded and roughly
    chopped
2 garlic cloves
1 large handful mint leaves, plus extra
    to serve
1 can (15-oz.) chickpeas, washed and
    drained
1 teaspoon ground cumin
2 tablespoons all-purpose flour
juice and zest of 1 lemon
4 tablespoons sesame seeds
2 tablespoons olive oil
sea salt and freshly ground black pepper

FOR THE DIP
scant 1 cup plain yogurt
3 tablespoons tahini paste
juice of ½ lemon

GOES WELL WITH
Fattoush Salad (page 33)
Lebanese Lemon and Vanilla Cake
    (page 198)

1 Put the onion, green chili, garlic and mint into a food processor and pulse for a few
seconds until everything is finely chopped. Add the chickpeas, cumin, flour, lemon
juice and zest and season with a really good pinch of salt and pepper. Blitz the lot
into a fairly smooth paste, tip into a bowl, cover and refrigerate 30 minutes.

2 To make the dip, mix the yogurt, tahini paste and lemon juice in a bowl, season
with a good pinch of salt and pepper and set aside.

3 Divide the falafel mixture into eight equal portions and mold into burger shapes.
Scatter the sesame seeds onto a plate and press a burger into the sesame seeds until
coated on all sides. Repeat with the remaining burgers.

4 Heat the oil in a skillet over medium heat, then fry the falafel 3 minutes on each side,
or until golden and crisp. Serve immediately with the tahini dip and a scattering
of mint leaves.

Huevos Mexicanos Mexican Scrambled Eggs

To learn about real Mexican food you have to go and stay with my wonderful friend Estella at her beautiful casa in the rolling hills of Puebla. She is such a character; so passionate about Mexican food and always wearing a cheeky smile on her face. On the first morning at Estella's casa, she gave me my first taste of real Mexican food—Huevos Mexicanos—which she served with warm tortillas. I stayed with my friend for a week, during which time she taught me my tomatillos from my tamales, my chili poblanos from my serranos and she passed on her passion for real Mexican cooking.

1 Heat the oil in a large skillet over medium heat, then add the onion, red pepper, garlic and green chili. Cook, stirring occasionally, 6 to 8 minutes until the onion turns golden. Add the tomatoes, mix well and cook 3 to 4 minutes longer until the tomatoes start to soften.

2 Tip in the eggs and season with a good pinch of salt and pepper. Mix well and leave for a minute or so until the eggs begin to set around the edge of the pan, then mix everything around until the eggs set completely.

3 Throw in the scallions and cilantro, give the scrambled eggs one final mix and serve immediately.

SERVES 2
2 tablespoons vegetable oil
1 small red onion, finely chopped
½ red bell pepper, seeded and finely chopped
1 garlic clove, finely chopped
½ green chili, seeded and finely chopped
2 tomatoes, finely chopped
4 extra-large eggs, beaten
2 scallions, finely chopped
1 small handful cilantro leaves
sea salt and freshly ground black pepper

GOES WELL WITH
Herb and Spice Pilaf Rice (page 181)
Mexican Cinnamon Peaches (page 206)

Garlic

Garlic is one of my favorite ingredients. Whether used in huge quantities in a curry or stir-fry, squished out of its skin from a bulb that's been roasted in the oven, rubbed raw all over a tomato bruschetta or simply mashed generously into mayonnaise, I love it.

This spice is cultivated all over the world, but China is the largest producer. It is still regarded as having excellent medicinal purposes, such as reducing cholesterol and high blood pressure or fighting off colds with its antibacterial properties. Due to its wonderful pungent flavor, garlic is even considered by some religions, such as the Jains, to be a stimulant, which warms the body thus increasing ones desires, and is avoided altogether.

We can get garlic in so many varieties: fresh, powdered, prechopped, pickled, pureed, smoked and even infused in oil. In its raw form, garlic has a wonderful sharp, peppery, pungent taste, which mellows and sweetens when cooked to add a real depth of flavor. Call me a purist, but I only ever recommend using the fresh stuff. It's so easy to prepare, lasts a good few weeks in a dry place and tastes much better than anything else.

The easiest way to prepare garlic is to take a clove and lay it flat onto a cutting board. Cut off the flat, stalky end and gently push down on the garlic using the flat side of the knife. This will cause the skin to break loose, so you can remove the clove easily. You can now thinly slice the clove as it is, or if you need to finely chop the garlic, bash the peeled clove again using the flat side of the knife to break it up more so it is easier to chop. At this stage you can also mash the garlic into a paste. To do this, simply add a pinch of sea salt to the already bashed garlic and rub it into the garlic using the flat side of a knife. Stop once you have a lovely smooth paste.

Cheese Quesadillas with a Green Mole Sauce

1 To make the green mole sauce, put all the ingredients into a food processor, season with a really good pinch of salt and pepper and blend on a high setting about 5 minutes, or until really smooth. Pour into a large saucepan and bring to a boil. Cover, reduce the heat to low and simmer, stirring occasionally, 30 minutes, or until the sauce reduces slightly and the flavors develop. The sauce will start to look a little grainy at this point, so pour it back into the blender and blend 30 seconds until beautifully smooth again. If using an upright blender, remember to leave a tiny gap in the lid so the steam can escape.

2 Heat a large skillet over medium heat and put in one of the tortillas. Lay one quarter of the mozzarella over the tortilla, then put another one over the top. Heat for about 2 minutes, or until the cheese starts to bubble out of the sides of the quesadillas and the bottom tortilla has started to crisp. Push the top of the quesadilla down with a spatula and then flip it over. Cook 2 minutes longer, or until the tortilla is crisp. Repeat with the remaining tortillas.

3 Cut each quesadilla into quarters and serve immediately with the Green Mole Sauce.

SERVES 4
8 large flour tortillas
10 ounces mozzarella, thinly sliced

FOR THE GREEN MOLE SAUCE
2 large handfuls parsley leaves
2 large handfuls cilantro leaves
2 large mild green chilies, seeded
4 scallions
juice of 2 limes
¼ cup pumpkin seeds
⅓ cup sesame seeds
2 garlic cloves
½ tablespoon cumin seeds
2 tablespoons olive oil
2¼ cups hot vegetable stock
sea salt and freshly ground black pepper

GOES WELL WITH
Feta, Walnut and Nigella Seed Salad
(page 21)
Asparagus, Green Bean and Wasabi
Salad (page 36)

Lebanese Pizza

In Beirut, I worked at a beautiful brasserie called Souk el Tayeb. Normally, I didn't eat breakfast because I ate so much and so well during the day. One morning, however, I was so hungry that I asked the guys for breakfast, which turned out to be my new "breakfast of champions": a freshly cooked flat bread, smothered in spices and filled with cheese and fresh mint. I was instructed to open it up and douse it with chili and lemon juice before tucking in. It was a wondrous culinary experience and here is my version.

SERVES 4

2 tablespoons dried thyme
1½ teaspoons ground cumin
½ teaspoon ground allspice
¼ teaspoon chili powder
4 tablespoons olive oil
4 large flour tortillas
7 ounces cherry tomatoes, halved
7 ounces mozzarella, thinly sliced
1 large handful mint leaves, roughly
    chopped
sea salt
lemon wedges, to serve

GOES WELL WITH

Fattoush Salad (page 33)
Tropical Fruit Salad with a Chili,
    Star Anise, Cinnamon and Lime
    Dressing (page 210)
Lemongrass and Ginger Rum Cocktail
    (page 216)

1 Preheat the oven to 425°F. Mix the thyme, cumin, allspice, chili powder, oil and a pinch of salt together in a bowl. Lay out the tortillas on an oven rack and brush the tops with the flavored oil. Divide the cherry tomatoes and mozzarella into four potions and arrange over the top of each tortilla.

2 Put the rack with the pizzas in the oven and cook 5 to 6 minutes until the bread becomes really crisp at the edges and the cheese melts. Scatter the mint leaves over and serve immediately with wedges of lemon to squeeze over the top.

Cambodian Street-Style Vegetable Curry

SERVES 4

2 tablespoons vegetable oil
1 red onion, roughly chopped
1¾ cups coconut cream
juice of 1 lime
3 tablespoons vegetarian fish sauce
1 zucchini, diced into bite-size pieces
3½ cups cremini mushrooms roughly
    chopped into bite-size pieces
2½ cups cauliflower florets broken into
    bite-size pieces
1½ red chilies, seeded and thinly sliced
1 cup frozen peas
1 handful cilantro leaves, roughly
    chopped

FOR THE CURRY PASTE

3 lemongrass stalks
3 garlic cloves
2 teaspoons ground coriander
½ teaspoon sugar

GOES WELL WITH

Rosamma's Crispy Chili Chicken
    (page 80)
Fried Steaks with Black Pepper Dip
    (page 88)
Herb and Spice Pilaf Rice (page 180)

1 To prepare the curry paste, remove the really tough outer leaves of the lemongrass and cut off the ends of the stalks. Starting at the fatter end, roughly slice each lemongrass stalk into rings. You should see a purple band in the rings. Stop slicing when there are no more purple bands, as the tops will be too tough to eat. Set the tops aside to add to the curry later and put the sliced lemongrass in a mini food processor. Add the other curry paste ingredients and blend to a smooth paste.

2 Heat the oil in a large saucepan over medium heat, then add the onion and fry, stirring occasionally, 6 to 8 minutes until beautifully golden and tender. Spoon in the curry paste and stir-fry 30 seconds, or until fragrant, then pour in the coconut cream, lime juice and fish sauce and chuck in the reserved lemongrass tops. Mix well and bring to a boil.

3 Add the zucchini, mushrooms, cauliflower and red chilies, then turn down the heat to low and simmer 15 minutes. Tip in the frozen peas, mix well and then cook over low heat 10 minutes longer, or until all the vegetables are tender but still have a little bite.

4 Remove the lemongrass tops from the curry and chuck in the cilantro. Mix well and serve immediately.

Charred Eggplants with Indian Spices and Cilantro

This is one of the best ways to use eggplants I've ever come across. There are different varieties of this dish, usually known as *baingan bharta*—mashed eggplant—all over India. This one is from Punjab. It's great served with any grilled or broiled meat or fish, or on its own as a dip. It also works hot, cold or at room temperature, so get cooking and see what you think.

1 If using a gas flame, turn your largest gas ring up to high. Using tongs, hold one of the eggplants over the flame 8 to 10 minutes, turning every 2 to 3 minutes, until the eggplant is nicely charred all over and soft and tender. Repeat with the remaining eggplants. If using the oven, preheat it to 400°F and roast the eggplants 45 minutes, turning every 15 minutes, or until charred and soft.

2 Wait for the eggplants to cool, then carefully remove the stems and peel off the charred skin using a sharp knife. Try to remove most of the skin, but don't worry about leaving the odd bit, as it will only add to the smoky flavor. Lightly mash the eggplant flesh into a rough paste with a fork.

3 Heat the oil in a large skillet over high heat, then add the onion and green chili. Stir-fry 3 to 4 minutes until golden, then add the tomatoes, turmeric, garam masala, coriander, salt and mashed eggplants. Mix well, cover, reduce the heat to low and simmer, stirring occasionally, 30 minutes. If the mixture starts to look dry, just add a splash of water.

4 Add the cilantro and lemon juice to freshen things up, mix well and serve hot, at room temperature or cold.

SERVES 4
2 large eggplants
2 tablespoons vegetable oil
1 large red onion, finely chopped
1 green chili, seeded and finely chopped
2 tomatoes, finely chopped
1 teaspoon turmeric
1 teaspoon garam masala
2 teaspoons ground coriander
1 teaspoon sea salt
1 large handful cilantro leaves, chopped
juice of ½ lemon

GOES WELL WITH
Chicken in Macadamia Nut and
   Mustard Seed Sauce (page 73)
Indian Spinach Cutlets with Raita
   (page 163)

Indian Spinach Cutlets with Raita

1 Put the potatoes in a large saucepan of water. Place over high heat and bring to a boil, then turn the heat down and simmer 15 to 20 minutes until tender. While the potatoes are cooking, place the spinach in a colander on top to steam 8 to 10 minutes until it completely wilts.

2 Drain the potatoes and mash until smooth. Once the spinach is cool squeeze out the excess moisture with your hands. This stops the cutlets from being soggy.

3 Heat 2 tablespoons of the oil in a skillet over medium heat, then stir-fry the onion, ginger and green chili 4 to 5 minutes until soft. Chuck in the pepper, garam masala and salt and cook 1 minute longer. Remove the pan from the heat and set aside to cool.

4 Meanwhile, mix the raita ingredients together in a bowl, season with a good pinch of salt and pepper and set aside.

5 Once everything has cooled to room temperature, put the mashed potato, spinach, onion mixture and flour in a bowl, mix well, cover and set aside 30 minutes.

6 Divide the mixture into four equal portions and shape each one into a flattened cutlet. Spread the breadcrumbs out on a plate and gently press a cutlet into the breadcrumbs until coated on both sides. Repeat with the remaining cutlets.

7 Heat the remaining 2 tablespoons of oil in a skillet over medium heat, then fry the cutlets 2 to 3 minutes on each side, or until golden and crisp. Serve immediately with the raita, sprinkled with ground cumin.

SERVES 4

7 ounces potatoes, peeled and cut into large chunks
14 ounces spinach, washed
4 tablespoons vegetable oil
1 large onion, finely chopped
1-inch piece gingerroot, peeled and finely chopped
1 green chili, seeded and finely chopped
1½ teaspoons freshly ground black pepper
1 teaspoon garam masala
1 teaspoon sea salt
2 tablespoons all-purpose flour
2 large handfuls dried breadcrumbs

FOR THE RAITA

1 cup plain yogurt
½ cucumber, seeded and finely chopped
juice of ½ lemon
1 small handful mint leaves
sea salt and freshly ground black pepper
ground cumin, to serve

GOES WELL WITH
Kerala Korma (page 68)
Red Lentil Dal (page 174)

Chana Masala **Indian Chickpeas**

For most people, Delhi is a place to land and leave: it's hot, busy and full on. My friend Ayesha, however, arranged for me to stay with her father in New Dehli and my experience was somewhat different. I was greeted at the airport by a stylish driver with an even more stylish Merc and driven to Ayesha's family home—fantastic. There were three chefs, and I spent every waking hour in the kitchen. The food was outstanding, and this chickpea dish is my version of something one of the chefs cooked for me.

SERVES 4

2 tablespoons vegetable oil
2 teaspoons cumin seeds
½ teaspoon sea salt
1 teaspoon ground coriander
½ teaspoon garam masala
½ teaspoon freshly ground black pepper
1 green chili, seeded and thinly sliced
2 cans (15-oz.) chickpeas, drained and
    rinsed
juice of 1 lemon, plus extra wedges
    to serve
½ red onion, thinly sliced
1 handful cilantro leaves, chopped
good-quality olive oil, to serve

GOES WELL WITH

Indian Chicken and Spinach Curry
    (page 70)
Golden Temple Lamb Curry
    (page 98)

1 Heat the vegetable oil in a large pan over medium heat, then add the cumin seeds. Let them crackle 10 seconds, then chuck in the salt, coriander, garam masala, black pepper and half the green chili. Fry, stirring constantly, a couple of seconds until fragrant.

2 Add the chickpeas, lemon juice and 1 cup and 2 tablespoons freshly boiled water, which should be enough to just cover everything. Gently mash some of the chickpeas with the back of a spoon to help the sauce thicken. Turn the heat up to high, bring to a boil and cook, stirring occasionally, 10 to 12 minutes until the sauce reduces right down and is very thick and just coating the chickpeas.

3 Throw in the onion, cilantro and the remaining green chili. This will give the dish a lovely fresh flavor and raw crunch. Mix everything together, drizzle some olive oil over and serve with wedges of lemon to squeeze over. This dish is also really delicious served chilled.

Sri Lankan Fried Potatoes

Sri Lankan food is a really interesting mix. It is a bit Southern Indian and a bit Malaysian meets Chinese food, which all sounds rather complicated. Basically, it is delicious. When in Sri Lanka, I spent a few days cooking in a town called Kandy with my hilarious teacher Priyani, who could not understand, why I, a man, wanted to know how to cook. Men don't cook in Sri Lanka. The whole family thought it so odd that, on my first day, they kept calling their friends to tell them a strange Western man was having cooking lessons in their house. The food we made was home cooking at its best. This is my version of Priyani's fried potatoes, which I am sure she would approve of; I'm sure she would also roar with laughter at the thought of me cooking it!

SERVES 4

1 pound waxy red potatoes, sliced into
    ½-inch-thick strips
2 tablespoons vegetable oil
1 large red onion, thinly sliced
1 cup halved cherry tomatoes
1 green chili, seeded and finely chopped
1 teaspoon garam masala
a large pinch of dried curry leaves
sea salt

GOES WELL WITH

Kerala Korma (page 68)
Steamed Cod in a Banana Leaf
    (page 126)

1 Put the potatoes in a large bowl, cover with cold water and set aside 10 minutes.
2 Meanwhile, heat the oil in a skillet over medium heat, then add the onions and stir-fry 8 to 9 minutes until golden. Drain the potatoes, then add to the skillet along with the tomatoes, green chili, garam masala and scant ½ cup hot water and season well with salt. Rub the curry leaves between your hands so they break up and chuck them into the skillet. Mix everything together until well combined, then bring to a boil, cover, reduce the heat to low and cook 15 minutes, or until the potatoes are tender.
3 Uncover and cook, stirring occasionally, 5 minutes longer, or until the liquid reduces and is just coating the potatoes. Serve immediately.

Crispy Szechuan Tofu

The base for this amazing Szechuan dish is the spice combination of the garlic, ginger, Szechuan pepper and chili flakes. They work like old friends who have reunited in a flavor explosion. To take the edge off this spicy mix, I've added soy sauce, for its saltiness, and scallions, which lift the flavors with their fresh fragrance. The crisp tofu, which begins to soften and soak up all the amazing flavors, is the perfect vehicle to carry such an explosive sauce, and the result is a dish that ignites every taste sensation in your mouth.

1 Heat the oil in a deep, heavy-bottom skillet over high heat. You need to make sure the oil is very hot so the tofu will be crisp, so test the temperature by carefully dropping in a tiny piece of tofu. If the oil is hot enough the tofu should immediately rise to the surface surrounded by bubbles and turn golden and crisp. Add the tofu to the pan in batches, 3 or 4 pieces at a time. Fry, turning the tofu pieces occasionally with a slotted spoon, 6 to 8 minutes until beautifully golden and crisp. Carefully remove the tofu with the spoon and place on paper towels to drain.

2 Mix the cornstarch, red wine vinegar, soy sauce and sugar together with a scant ½ cup water in a small bowl. Heat a wok over high heat, then add the tablespoon of oil. Once the oil is hot, add the ginger, garlic, scallions, Szehucan pepper and chili flakes. Stir-fry 10 seconds, or until fragrant, then reduce the heat to medium and add the cornstarch mixture. Mix everything really well and continue to stir-fry 2 minutes, or until the sauce reduces and is really thick. Add the tofu and gently mix together.

3 Turn the heat to low and cook 1 to 2 minutes until heated through. Serve immediately.

SERVES 4

2 cups plus 2 tablespoons vegetable oil, plus 1 tablespoon for stir-frying
12 ounces firm tofu, drained and sliced into ½-inch-thick cubes
½ tablespoon cornstarch
1 tablespoon red wine vinegar
2 tablespoons soy sauce
1 teaspoon sugar
1-inch piece gingerroot, peeled and finely chopped
4 garlic cloves, finely chopped
6 scallions, finely chopped
½ teaspoon ground Szechuan pepper
½ teaspoon chili flakes

GOES WELL WITH
Fried Steaks with Black Pepper Dip (page 88)
Sri Lankan Deviled Monkfish (page 117)

Beijing Teahouse Vegetable Stir-Fry

I got my inspiration for this delicious dish at a restaurant called Han Cang, in the Xicheng district of Beijing, where I ate lunch with friends one memorable fall day. We walked there via the beautiful complex of lakes that spread out from The Forbidden Palace, over ornate Chinese bridges with brown and orange leaves drifting gently underneath and past the rows of government exercise bikes and cross trainers that line the banks of the lakes. Amazing! Lunch was a taste of real China. We had sweet-and-sour fish, beef hot pot and a lovely stir-fried mushroom dish. This is my version of that memorable stir-fry.

1 Heat a large wok over high heat and add the oil. Once it is smoking hot, remove the wok from the heat and add the Szechuan peppercorns. Stir in the hot oil 30 seconds, then remove them with a slotted spoon. This will give you all their spicy numbing flavor without leaving behind any gritty bits.

2 Reheat the wok over high heat. Once smoking hot again, add the garlic, ginger, onion and chili flakes and stir-fry 1 to 2 minutes until everything starts to turn golden. Add the mushrooms and stir-fry 2 minutes longer, or until they start to wilt and take on a little color, then add the bok choy and stir-fry 2 minutes until it starts to soften. Pour in the soy sauce and oyster sauce and stir-fry 1 minute longer, or until everything is coated in the rich juices and piping hot.

SERVES 4

2 tablespoons vegetable oil
1 teaspoon Szechuan peppercorns
3 garlic cloves, sliced lengthwise
1-inch piece gingerroot, peeled
    and finely chopped
1 red onion, finely chopped
1 teaspoon chili flakes
9 ounces oyster mushrooms, torn
    in smaller pieces
7 ounces pak choi, cut in half
2 tablespoons soy sauce
1 tablespoon vegetarian oyster sauce

GOES WELL WITH

Stir-Fried Beef with Black Pepper and
    Basil (page 89)
Twice-Cooked Pork (page 111)

Cambodian Roasted Eggplants with Ginger and Coconut

Like many Cambodian dishes, these eggplants have a mix of Thai and Chinese flavors. It works beautifully, with the tender chunks of roasted eggplant soaking up the creamy coconut sauce. The main spice here is black pepper, which is often used in Cambodian cooking instead of chili—add an extra half teaspoon if you want an extra kick.

SERVES 4
1 tablespoon vegetable oil
2 large eggplants
2 tablespoons shredded coconut
2-inch piece gingerroot, peeled and thinly sliced
2 cups coconut cream
2 tablespoons oyster sauce
1 teaspoon freshly ground black pepper
a large pinch of sugar
4 scallions, thinly sliced

GOES WELL WITH:
Broiled Lamb Skewers with a Bulgur Wheat Salad (page 106)
Indian Fish Cakes with a Cilantro and Coconut Chutney (page 122)
Malasian Spice Garden Shrimp Curry (page 138)

1 Preheat the oven to 400°F. Rub the oil over the skin of the eggplants, then transfer them to a roasting tray and roast 25 to 30 minutes until soft but not cooked to a pulp. Once they are cool enough to handle, peel off the skin and chop the soft flesh into large chunks.

2 Heat a shallow skillet over medium heat, then add the coconut and ginger. Stir-fry 2 to 3 minutes, stirring continuously, until the coconut starts turning golden. Pour in the coconut cream, oyster sauce, black pepper and sugar and mix well. Bring to a boil and add the cooked eggplant. Reduce the heat to low and simmer 5 minutes until the eggplant is warmed through and the sauce slightly reduces. Scatter the scallions over and serve immediately.

Gobi Masala Indian Stir-Fried Cauliflower

The reason this cauliflower dish works so well is because it relies only on a few simple ingredients. The onion, tomato and ginger provide the base for the whole dish and the cauliflower the main flavor. A little chili powder and garam masala is all it takes to give a lovely, spicy taste, while the cilantro freshens things up at the end. This dish is delicious on its own as well as part of a larger meal with lots of other delicious things.

SERVES 4
2 tablespoons vegetable oil
1 large onion, finely chopped
2-inch piece gingerroot, peeled
    and cut into matchsticks
2 tomatoes, finely chopped
4½ cups cauliflower florets cut into
    bite-size pieces
½ teaspoon chili powder
1 teaspoon garam masala
1 teaspoon sea salt
1 large handful cilantro leaves, roughly
    chopped
naan bread, to serve

GOES WELL WITH
Indian Chicken and Spinach Curry
    (page 70)
Roast Lebanese Leg of Lamb with
    Spiced Lentil Puree (page 97)

1 Heat the oil in a large skillet over high heat. Add the onion and stir-fry 3 to 4 minutes until golden, then add the ginger and tomatoes and stir-fry 1 minute longer.

2 Add the cauliflower, chili powder, garam masala, salt and scant ½ cup hot water and mix well. Bring to a boil, then cover, reduce the heat to low and simmer 20 to 25 minutes until the cauliflower is tender but still has a little bite. Throw in the cilantro, mix well and serve with naan bread.

Red Lentil Dal

SERVES 4

1 cup split red lentils, washed and
drained
2 tablespoons vegetable oil
2 teaspoons cumin seeds
1 red onion, finely chopped
1-inch piece gingerroot, peeled and
sliced into thin matchsticks
1 green chili, seeded and finely chopped
2 tomatoes, finely chopped
2 teaspoons sea salt
1 teaspoon turmeric
2 teaspoons ground coriander
chopped cilantro leaves, to serve
rice, to serve

GOES WELL WITH

Coconut and Ginger Chicken Stir-Fry
(page 54)
Za'atar Lamb Cutlets (page 104)
Shrimp with Ginger and Chili
(page 139)

1 Put the lentils into a saucepan with 3 cups water. Bring to a boil and then turn the heat down to low, cover and simmer 15 to 20 minutes until the lentils absorb all the water and are tender. Check them every couple of minutes after the 15-minute mark to make sure they aren't burning.

2 Heat a wok over medium heat and add the oil. Once the oil is hot, chuck in the cumin seeds and let them crackle a few seconds. Add the onion, ginger and green chili and stir-fry, stirring occasionally, 3 to 4 minutes until the onion is soft and golden.

3 Add the tomatoes, salt, turmeric, coriander and 3 tablespoons water. Reduce the heat to low and cook, stirring occasionally, 8 to 10 minutes until the tomatoes break down into a thick sauce.

4 Pour the tomato sauce into the lentils and mix everything together. Scatter the cilantro over the top and serve immediately with rice.

Frijoles Negros

Mexican Refried Beans with Garlic, Chili and Cilantro

In Mexico, almost every dish in every restaurant at every meal, comes with beans, and you'll find a huge pot of *frijoles negros* simmering in kitchens all over Mexico, waiting to be mashed and then fried to make this beloved dish.

1 Put the beans in a large saucepan of water with the baking soda. Mix well and leave 2 hours. This makes the beans more digestible. Drain, rinse and return the beans to the saucepan with 3½ cups water. Add the quartered onion, green chili, peppercorns and the whole garlic cloves. Turn the heat up to high and bring to a boil, then cover, reduce the heat to low and simmer 2 hours 30 minutes.

2 Uncover the saucepan, turn the heat up to medium and cook the beans, stirring occasionally, 30 to 40 minutes until they are beautifully tender and the sauce reduces right down and is really thick. Season with a really good pinch of salt and mix everything together. Transfer to a large mixing bowl and mash until the beans start to break down. I like them to still have some texture, but you can make them as smooth as you like.

3 Heat the oil in a large skillet over high heat and add the chopped onion, sliced garlic cloves and the jalapeño chile. Stir-fry 3 to 4 minutes until the onion and garlic are lovely and golden. Add the beans to the pan, mix well and reduce the heat to medium. Cook 4 to 5 minutes until heated through and very creamy in texture.

4 Mix in the scallions, lime juice, cilantro and a final pinch of salt and pepper. Serve immediately with loads of tortilla chips for dipping.

SERVES 4

1 cup black beans
1 teaspoon baking soda
2 red onions, 1 quartered and 1 finely chopped
1 green chili, slit open at the bottom
10 black peppercorns
6 garlic cloves, 4 whole and 2 sliced
2 tablespoons olive oil
1 red jalapeño chile, seeded and roughly chopped
4 scallions, finely chopped
juice of 1 lime
2 large handfuls cilantro leaves, finely chopped
sea salt and freshly ground black pepper
tortilla chips, to serve

GOES WELL WITH

Shredded Beef Tacos (page 86)
Estella's Mexican Beef-Filled Peppers with a Pecan Sauce (page 92)

CHAPTER SIX

Rice and Noodles

Why settle for the same old boring rice? In this chapter
I will show you how easy it is to cook a load of wonderful
rice dishes using a few simple spices. A little cardamom and
cumin with a few fresh herbs is all it takes to make Herb
and Spice Pilaf Rice, for   example, which is one of my
favorite rice dishes to serve with any grilled or broiled
meat, fish or vegetable. Adding whole spices to rice lends
so much flavor without you really doing anything. Chucking
in some cinnamon, cloves, star anise and cardamom gives an
immense amount of flavor to the Tomato and Coconut Rice.
And the same applies to noodles; they soak up all the flavor
of the spices, so a little goes a long way. For example, by
adding garam masala, turmeric and fresh chili to make Surf
and Turf Noodles, you will transform what would otherwise
be a bland stir-fry into something vibrant and delicious.

LEFT: Char Kueh Toew (page 193)

Veracruz Rice with Seafood

The strong flavors of this Mexican-inspired dish come from the delicious aromas and flavors of the cinnamon and cloves. These permeate the rice as it cooks in the sauce giving it depth. The garlic and tomatoes provide balance, and the cilantro and fresh lime juice, added just before serving, lift the rich, spice flavors that combine superbly with juicy jumbo shrimp.

SERVES 4

2 tablespoons olive oil
1 onion, finely chopped
1 can (15-oz.) crushed tomatoes
1 red chili, seeded and finely chopped
2 garlic cloves
2-inch piece cinnamon stick
3 cloves
½ teaspoon sugar
1¾ cups basmati rice
2½ cups chicken or vegetable stock
8 raw jumbo shrimp, shells on
1 handful cilantro leaves, roughly
    chopped
juice of 1 lime
sea salt and freshly ground black pepper
1 lime, quartered, to serve

GOES WELL WITH

Mexican Chicken with Yogurt and
    Almonds (page 75)
Indian Seekh Kebabs (page 105)

1 Heat the oil in a large skillet over medium heat, then add the onion and fry, stirring occasionally, 6 to 8 minutes until the onion turns golden. Add the tomatoes, red chili, garlic, cinnamon, cloves and sugar and season with a good pinch of salt and pepper. Mix well and bring to a boil, then cover, reduce the heat to low and simmer 10 minutes.

2 Meanwhile, put the rice into a large saucepan, cover with cold water and stir, then set aside 5 minutes to soak. Tip the rice into a colander and give it a really good rinse under running cold water until the water coming out of the rice is clear. This washes the starch out of the rice and makes sure you get lovely, separated grains.

3 Tip the washed rice back into the saucepan and place over medium heat. Add the tomatoes and hot stock and gently mix together. Bring to a boil, then cover, reduce the heat to low and simmer 2 minutes.

4 Place the shrimp on top of the rice, put the lid back on the saucepan and cook 10 to 12 minutes until all the water is absorbed and the rice is almost cooked but still has some bite. Remove the pan from the heat and remove the lid. Place a clean dish towel over the rice, then replace the lid and set aside to steam 5 to 10 minutes.

5 Remove the cooked shrimp from the rice and set aside. Add the cilantro and lime juice to the rice, season with a really good pinch of salt and pepper and mix well. Place the shrimp back on the rice and serve immediately with the lime wedges.

Herb and Spice Pilaf Rice

1 Heat a large skillet over medium heat. Add the cashew nuts and gently toast, shaking the pan constantly, 1 to 2 minutes. Add the almonds and continue to shake the pan 1 to 2 minutes longer until both the cashew nuts and almonds start turning golden. Transfer the nuts to a plate and set aside.

2 Put the cardamom pods on a cutting board and, using the flat side of a knife, press down until they split open and reveal their seeds. This helps to release their flavor. Heat the oil in a large skillet over medium heat, then add the split cardamom pods and the cumin seeds. Stir-fry 10 to 20 seconds until the seeds start to crackle, then add the onion and continue stir-frying, stirring occasionally, 3 to 4 minutes until the onion is soft.

3 Put the rice into a large saucepan, cover with cold water and stir, then set aside 5 minutes to soak. Tip the rice into a colander and give it a really good rinse under running cold tap, until the water coming out of the rice is clear. This washes the starch out of the rice and makes sure you get lovely, separated grains.

4 Tip the washed rice back into the saucepan and place over medium heat. Add the onion and spice mixture and stir in the hot stock. Bring to a boil, cover, reduce the heat to low and simmer 10 to 15 minutes until all the water is absorbed and the rice is almost cooked but still has a little bite. Remove the pan from the heat and remove the lid. Place a clean dish towel over the rice, replace the lid and set aside to steam 5 to 10 minutes.

5 Fluff up the rice with a fork and toss together with the toasted nuts, parsley and cilantro. Season with a really good pinch of salt and pepper, drizzle a little oil over, add a few cilantro sprigs as a finishing touch and serve hot or warm.

SERVES 4
½ cup slivered almonds
⅓ cup cashew nuts
2 cardamom pods
2 tablespoons olive oil, plus extra for drizzling
2 teaspoons cumin seeds
1 large onion, finely chopped
1¾ cups basmati rice
2½ cups chicken or vegetable stock
2 large handfuls parsley leaves, finely chopped
2 large handfuls cilantro leaves, finely chopped, plus extra sprigs to serve
sea salt and freshly ground black pepper

GOES WELL WITH
Moroccan Lemon Chicken (page 67)
Persian Saffron and Honey Lamb Stew (page 101)
Sri Lankan Deviled Monkfish (page 117)

Sri Lankan Fried Rice with Cashew Nuts and Egg

SERVES 4

1¾ cups basmati rice
2-inch piece cinnamon stick
4 cloves
4 cardamom pods
1 teaspoon turmeric
1 teaspoon sea salt
3 tablespoons butter
1 large carrot, grated or finely chopped
1 red chili, seeded and finely chopped
½ cup cashew nuts
2 eggs, beaten
6 scallions, thinly sliced lengthwise and
    roughly chopped

GOES WELL WITH

Pueblan Almond Duck (page 82)
Golden Temple Lamb Curry
    (page 98)
Sri Lankan Deviled Monkfish
    (page 117)

1 Put the rice into a large saucepan, cover with cold water and stir well, then set aside 5 minutes to soak. Tip the rice into a colander and give it a really good rinse under tunning cold water until the water coming out of the rice is clear. This washes the starch out of the rice and make sure you get lovely, separated grains.

2 Tip the washed rice back into the saucepan and place over medium heat. Add the cinnamon, cloves, cardamom, turmeric, salt and 2½ cups hot water and mix until well combined. Bring to a boil, then cover, reduce the heat to low and simmer 10 to 15 minutes until all the water is absorbed and the rice is almost cooked but still has a little bite. Remove the pan from the heat and uncover. Place a clean dish towel over the rice, then replace the lid and set aside to steam 5 to 10 minutes.

3 Meanwhile, melt the butter in a large wok over medium heat. Once melted and hot, add the carrots and red chili and stir-fry 5 to 6 minutes until the carrot is soft. Add the cashew nuts and stir-fry 1 minute, then pour over the eggs and stir-fry 2 to 3 minutes longer until the eggs are cooked through.

4 Add the cooked rice and scallions to the wok and mix well with a fork, fluffing up the rice as you go. Serve immediately.

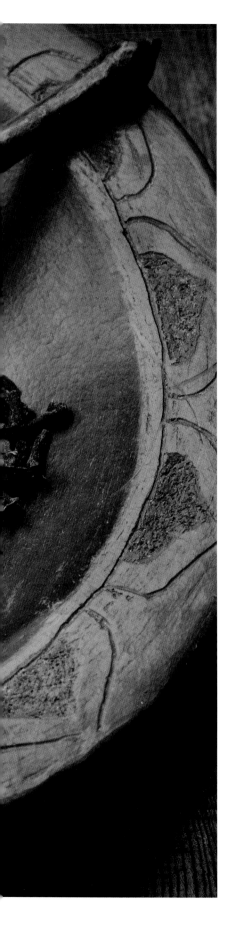

Cloves

I remember cloves from when I was younger, studded into hams and onions, which filled the kitchen with such a strong smell around Christmas time. I associated them with an old-fashioned style of cooking that didn't interest me. As I learned more about Indian food, however, I developed a new appreciation for this wonderful spice—either ground into the earthy garam masala spice mix or chucked into hot oil with other whole spices like cinnamon and black peppercorns and bay leaves. I suddenly noticed how amazing this little spice was and, as I cooked my way around the world, realized its full potential: five spice in China, curries and rice in Malaysia and Indonesia, slow-cooked Mexican sauces and even perfumed Moroccan spice blends.

What a history! The clove was one of the original trading spices of the sixteenth and seventeenth centuries, prized by the East India Trading Company and worth more than gold. The Dutch found their way to the Moluccas islands of Indonesia and seized control of the clove trade. To ensure its tight production, they ruthlessly burned clove trees that grew on other islands, which caused a massive loss of life to the native inhabitants. In 1755, however, one have-a-go Frenchman, Peter Poive, managed to smuggle one of the plants from the Dutch and planted his illegal crop in Mauritius, opening up the trade forever.

The clove is actually the unripened flower of a tree. The beautiful little flowers are picked when they are still hard and dried into the woody, brown-colored things we have in our kitchens. They have a big flavor and can overpower a dish if used too liberally. But used correctly, in both sweet and savory dishes, the clove adds the most amazing sweet, woody, almost dark chocolatelike, rich flavor and aroma. Whole cloves work best in dishes when they can be easily removed after they've imparted their flavor.

The whole spice will last up to a year, in a dry, airtight container that is kept out of any direct sunlight. Cloves are hard to grind into a powder, so it's worth keeping some of the ground spice on hand to add to curry powders, spice rubs or desserts. The flavor is still just as strong, but it will only last about six months, so it's best to buy in small amounts.

Nasi Goreng   Indonesian Fried Rice

Nasi Goreng is a classic rice dish that is served all over Indonesia and is also common in Malaysia and Singapore. It's usually served with a soft fried egg on the top—the best bit is breaking the yolk over the rice! This recipe calls for shrimp paste, which is a common ingredient in Southeast Asian cooking. The paste smells like death on its own, but adding a little bit while cooking adds the most amazing depth of flavor. If you can't get hold of any shrimp paste, use one tablespoon of fish sauce instead.

SERVES 4
3 tablespoons vegetable oil
1 onion, finely chopped
5 cups cold cooked rice
3 tablespoons soy sauce
4 eggs

FOR THE SPICE PASTE
¼ teaspoon shrimp paste
1 red bell pepper, seeded and roughly
    chopped
3 garlic cloves
1 red chili, seeded and roughly chopped
a pinch of sugar
1 teaspoon garam masala

GOES WELL WITH
Rosamma's Crispy Chili Chicken
    (page 80)

1   To make the spice paste, put all the ingredients into a mini food processor and blend until smooth.

2   Heat a wok over high heat, then add 2 tablespoons of the oil and heat until the oil is smoking. Chuck in the onion and stir-fry 3 to 4 minutes until golden. Tip in the spice paste and stir-fry 30 seconds, or until fragrant, then add the cooked rice and soy sauce and stir-fry, stirring continuously, 4 to 5 minutes longer until the rice is warmed through.

3   Meanwhile, heat the remaining 1 tablespoon of oil in a small skillet over medium heat and fry the eggs, carefully spooning the hot oil over them to make sure the white is cooked through but the yoke remains runny.

4   Divide the rice onto four serving plates, place the fried eggs on top of the rice and serve immediately.

Tomato and Coconut Rice

1 Put the rice into a large saucepan, cover with cold water, stir and set aside 5 minutes to soak. Tip the rice into a colander and give it a really good rinse under cold running water until the water coming out of the rice runs clear. This washes the starch out of the rice and makes ure you get lovely, separated grains.

2 Tip the washed rice back into the saucepan and place over medium heat. Add the coconut milk, cinnamon, star anise, cardamom, cloves, tomatoes and 1¾ cups hot water. Bring to a boil, then cover, reduce the heat to low and simmer10 to 15 minutes until all the liquid is absorbed and the rice is almost cooked but still has a little bite. Remove the pan from the heat and uncover. Place a clean dish towel over the rice, then replace the lid and set aside to steam 5 to 10 minutes.

3 Meanwhile, heat the oil in a skillet over medium heat. Add the shallots and fry 6 to 8 minutes until golden and crisp. Remove the shallots from the oil with a slotted spoon and set aside on paper towels to drain.

4 Season the cooked rice with salt, fluffing up the rice with a fork as you go. Sprinkle the fried shallots over and serve immediately.

SERVES 4

1¾ cups basmati rice
¾ cup coconut milk
1-inch cinnamon stick
1 star anise
2 cardamom pods
4 cloves
2 large tomatoes, finely chopped
2 tablespoons vegetable oil
5 shallots, thinly sliced
sea salt

GOES WELL WITH

Pomegranate, Fennel, Orange and
    Watercress Salad (page 22)
Indian Seekh Kebabs (page 105)
Malasian Spice Garden Shrimp Curry
    (page 138)

Lebanese Rice with Lamb and Eggplants

SERVES 4

4 tablespoons olive oil, plus extra
    for brushing
1 large eggplant, cut lengthwise into
    ¼-inch-thick strips
⅔ cup pine nuts
10 ounces ground lamb
1 onion, finely chopped
2 garlic cloves, finely chopped
2 large tomatoes, finely chopped
2-inch piece cinnamon stick
¼ teaspoons ground allspice
1¾ cups basmati rice
sea salt and freshly ground black pepper

GOES WELL WITH

Ciya Shish Kebab (page 94)
Roast Lebanese Leg of Lamb with
    Spiced Lentil Puree (page 97)
Al Pastor Pork and Pineapple Salad
    (page 110)

1   Brush a little oil on both sides of the eggplant slices. Heat a griddle pan over high heat until smoking. Add the eggplants and griddle 2 to 3 minutes on each side until tender and covered in lovely charred griddle lines. Set aside.

2   Heat a skillet over medium heat. Add the pine nuts and gently toast, shaking the pan occasionally, 2 to 3 minutes until the pine nuts are golden brown. Transfer the nuts to a plate and set aside.

3   Heat 2 tablespoons of the oil in a large skillet over medium heat, then add the lamb, onion and garlic. Fry 10 to 12 minutes until the lamb starts to color, stirring occassionally. Add the tomatoes, cinnamon and allspice, season with a good pinch of salt and pepper and cook 5 to 6 minutes longer until the tomatoes start to break down.

4   Put the rice into a large bowl, cover with cold water, stir and set aside 5 minutes to soak. Tip the rice into a colander and give it a really good rinse under cold running water until the water coming out of the rice runs clear. This washes the starch out of the rice and makes sure you get lovely, separated grains.

5   Tip the washed rice into the skillet and place over medium heat. Add the spiced lamb and stir in 2½ cups freshly boiled water. Bring to a boil, cover, reduce the heat to low and simmer 10 to 15 minutes until all the water is absorbed and the rice is almost cooked but still has a little bite. Scatter half the toasted pine nuts over and mix everything together with a fork, fluffing the rice as you go.

6   Meanwhile, preheat the oven to 350°F. Drizzle the bottom of a baking dish with a little oil. Arrange half the charred eggplants across the bottom of the dish, spread all of the rice and lamb mixture on top and then lay the other half of the eggplants on top of the rice. Scatter the remaining toasted pine nuts over and drizzle with a little more oil. Cover with foil and bake 10 minutes. Serve immediately.

Szechuan Noodles with Lamb and Peanuts

SERVES 4

9 ounces egg noodles
4 tablespoons vegetable oil
⅓ cup unsalted peanuts
½ teaspoon chili flakes
1 teaspoon Szechuan peppercorns
2 garlic cloves, finely chopped
1-inch piece gingerroot, peeled and
    finely chopped
7 ounces lamb steak or tenderloin,
    thinly sliced
1 leek, thinly sliced lengthwise
1 tablespoon oyster sauce
2 tablespoons light soy sauce

GOES WELL WITH

Chinese Pork Dumpling Soup
    (page 15)
Cambodian Caramelized Ginger
    Bananas with Vanilla Ice Cream
    (page 212)

1 Cook the noodles according to the package directions. Drain, drizzle with
   2 tablespoons of the oil to prevent the noodles from sticking and set aside.

2 Heat a wok over high heat and add the remaining oil. Once the oil is smoking hot,
   add the peanuts, chili flakes, Szechuan peppercorns, garlic and ginger and stir-fry
   10 seconds, or until fragrant. Add the lamb and leek and stir-fry 3 to 4 minutes until
   everything turns golden brown and the lamb is beautifully tender but still a little pink
   in the middle.

3 Use a knife to cut through the noodles a couple of times, then tip them into the wok.
   Cutting the noodles helps them to mix with the other ingredients. Pour the oyster
   sauce and soy sauce over and mix together well until the noodles are completely
   coated and warmed through. Serve immediately.

Surf and Turf Noodles

This is my version of Singapore noodles. Instead of a generic curry powder, I use a mixture of garam masala, turmeric and fresh chili, which provide the "curry" flavor, madly yellow color and lively, fresh heat. I also add an American "surf-and-turf" twist, using filet mignon and jumbo shrimp rather than the traditional pork char siu, which is a bit sweet. The spices work well together, and the soy sauce really accentuates their flavors.

SERVES 4

9 ounces thin rice noodles
4 tablespoons vegetable oil
½ onion, thinly sliced
3½ ounces filet mignon, thinly sliced
5 ounces jumbo shrimp, shelled and
   deveined
½ green bell pepper, seeded and finely
   chopped
6 scallions, roughly sliced
½ red chili, seeded and thinly sliced
1 teaspoon garam masala
½ teaspoon turmeric
2 tablespoons soy sauce

GOES WELL WITH

Guyi Cumin, Chili and Soy Ribs
   (page 112)
Creamy Cilantro Swordfish with a Red
   Onion Raita (page 123)

1 Cook the noodles according to the package directions. Drain well, then drizzle with 2 tablespoons of the oil to prevent the noodles from sticking and set aside.

2 Heat a large wok over high heat and add the remaining oil. Once the oil is smoking, add the onion and stir-fry 1 minute. Add the filet and shrimp and stir-fry 1 minute until the shrimp are starting to turn pink. Add the green pepper, scallions and red chili and continue stir-frying 1 minute longer, or until all the shrimp are completely pink and cooked through.

3 Use a knife to cut up the cooked noodles a couple of times, then tip them into the wok. Cutting the noodles helps them to mix with the other ingredients. Add the garam masala, turmeric and soy sauce and stir-fry 2 to 3 minutes until well combined and warmed through. Serve immediately.

Char Kueh Toew
Fried Rice Noodles with Shrimp and Egg

1 Cook the noodles according to the package directions. Drain well, then drizzle with 2 tablespoons of the oil to prevent them from sticking and set aside.

2 Put the red chili and garlic in a mini food processor and blend to a rough paste. Heat a wok over high heat and add the remaining 2 tablespoons of oil. Once the oil is smoking, add the chili paste and stir-fry 5 seconds, or until fragrant. Add the shrimp, scallions and sugar and stir-fry 2 to 3 minutes until the shrimp turn pink and are cooked through.

3 Use a knife to cut up the noodles a couple of times, then tip them into the wok. Cutting the noodles helps them to mix with the other ingredients. Pour the oyster sauce and soy sauce over and mix together well until the noodles are completely coated and warmed through.

4 Clear some space in the pan by pushing the noodles to one side. Pour the beaten eggs into the space you've created and stir-fry the eggs until they scramble. Mix the eggs with the noodles and serve immediately.

SERVES 4

9 ounces rice noodles
4 tablespoons vegetable oil
1 red chili, seeded and roughly chopped
2 garlic cloves
9 ounces raw shrimp, shelled and deveined
6 scallions, thinly sliced
a pinch of sugar
2 tablespoons oyster sauce
1 tablespoon soy sauce
2 eggs, beaten

GOES WELL WITH

Gung Bao Chicken (page 60)
Stir-Fried Beef with Black Pepper and Basil (page 89)
Alleppy Shrimp Curry (page 136)

CHAPTER SEVEN

Desserts and Drinks

Spices most definitely don't just belong in savory dishes —they can be used to make the most amazing desserts and drinks. In this decadent chapter I show you how simmering a few complementary spices together in a sugar syrup, for example, imparts a beautiful flavor that is the perfect way to end a meal. A little cinnamon is all it takes to make Mexican Cinnamon Peaches, and the same sweet cinnamon combined with a little star anise and chili creates the most exciting spicy sugar syrup for a Tropical Fruit Salad. Chocolate and spices are old friends and you will see how adding a few of my favorite spices brings out the flavor of the chocolate and creates an aroma that will have people knocking your door down to get at the Mayan Hot Chocolate or Dark Chocolate, Clove and Cinnamon Brownies. And adding the right spices to a cocktail lifts all the flavors of the drink into a party showstopper. A little fresh chili is the only spice needed to give a real twist to Chili Passionfruit Martini—a seriously grown up drink I know you will love.

LEFT: Lebanese Lemon and Vanilla Cake (page 198)

Dark Chocolate, Clove and Cinnamon Brownies

MAKES 16

2¼ cups unsalted butter, plus extra
    for greasing
10 ounces chocolate with 70 to 80%
    cocoa, plus extra to serve
heaped ½ cup granulated sugar
packed ⅔ cup soft light Demerara sugar
3 eggs and 1 egg yolk, beaten
1 cup pecan nuts, crushed
½ cup all-purpose flour
1 teaspoon baking powder
1 teaspoon sea salt
⅔ cup unsweetened cocoa powder, plus
    extra to serve
¼ teaspoon ground cloves
½ teaspoon ground cinnamon, plus
    extra to serve

GOES WELL WITH

Shrimp and Lemongrass Rice Noodle
    Salad (page 46)
Mexican Chicken with Yogurt and
    Almonds (page 75)
Persian Saffron and Honey Lamb
    Stew (page 101)

1 Preheat the oven to 350°F. Grease the bottom and sides of a 9-inch square cake pan, then line with baking parchment.

2 Break the chocolate into pieces and melt it in a heatproof bowl set over a saucepan of barely simmering water. Make sure the bottom of the bowl doesn't touch the water. Once completely melted, set the chocolate aside to cool slightly.

3 Put the butter, granulated sugar and Demerara sugar into a food processor and blend on a high setting about 5 minutes, or until they form a smooth paste.

4 Slowly add the eggs, a little at a time, to the butter and sugar mixture and blend on a low setting until everything is incorporated. Give the mixture a final blast on a high setting 30 seconds, then transfer to a large mixing bowl.

5 Slowly fold in the melted chocolate, then add the nuts and sift in the flour, baking powder, salt, cocoa powder, cloves and cinnamon. Fold everything together using a large metal spoon, then scrape the batter into the prepared cake pan. Smooth the top with a metal spatula and bake 20 to 30 minutes until soft and gooey in the middle and just cracking on the top and sides. To test if the brownie is baked through, insert a skewer into the middle, pushing right to the bottom. It should come out with a little of the yummy, gooey brownie clinging but not totally coating it. If the skewer is completely coated, put the brownie back in the oven and test it again every 3 minutes until baked.

6 Remove the pan from the oven and leave the brownie to cool 30 minutes in the pan. Flip the brownie out of the pan onto a cutting board, peel off the baking parchment and cut into squares. Serve hot, warm or cold with a generous sprinkling of cocoa powder and a sprinkling of cinnamon, to taste.

Lebanese Lemon and Vanilla Cake

SERVES 8 TO 10
5 unwaxed lemons
1½ cups granulated sugar
1¾ sticks unsalted butter
1 vanilla bean
3 eggs
1¼ cups all-purpose flour
crème fraîche, to serve

GOES WELL WITH
Pomegranate, Fennel, Orange and
    Watercress Salad (page 22)
Broiled Haddock, Apple and Cilantro
    Salad with a Lemongrass Dressing
    (page 43)
Stir-Fried Squid with Chili and
    Cilantro (page 145)

1 Preheat the oven to 350°F. Cut 3 of the lemons into thin slices and remove any seeds. Zest one of the remaining 2 lemons, and then squeeze the juice from both of them.

2 Heat a large, heavy-bottom skillet over medium heat, then sprinkle heaped ½ cup of the sugar over the bottom in an even layer. After a few moments the edge of the sugar should start to melt, at which time give the pan a good shake, then leave it until half of the sugar turns to liquid. Stir the sugar with a wooden spoon until all the sugar is completely caramelized and clear. Carefully pour the caramel into an 8-inch nonstick cake pan, covering the bottom completely. Lay the lemon slices on top of the caramel, starting around the edges and working toward the middle.

3 Melt the butter in a small saucepan over low heat, then set aside to cool slightly.

4 Using a sharp knife, split the vanilla bean in half and scrape out the seeds. Put the seeds in a food processor with the eggs and the remaining sugar. Blend 10 to 12 minutes on a high setting until the mixture doubles in volume and is very light in color. Transfer to a large mixing bowl and fold in the melted butter and lemon zest and juice with a large metal spoon. Sift the flour over in small batches, folding it in as you go. Once the batter is completely blended and smooth, pour it into the cake pan over the lemons.

5 Bake 30 minutes, or until the cake is risen and is soft enough to leave a fingerprint on the top. A skewer inserted into the middle of the cake should come out clean.

6 Remove the pan from the oven, place a serving plate on top and confidently flip it over. Give the bottom of the cake pan a few knocks with a heavy spoon, then gently lift it up to reveal the cake and the lovely caramel. Leave the cake to cool at least 1 hour, then serve with the crème fraîche.

Steamed Ginger Custard Pots

Sometimes less is more! These silky smooth steamed puddings are brought to life by the addition of one spice—fresh, peppery ginger. The whole pudding is transformed from a simple steamed custard into a really sophisticated dish. It's very light and is the perfect palate cleanser after a spicy meal.

1 Put the milk and sugar in a mixing bowl and whisk until all the sugar dissolves, then pour in the eggs and whisk to combine. Grate the ginger over the bowl, discarding any fibrous parts, and whisk again until all the ingredients are well combined.

2 Strain the mixture into a pouring jug, then pour the mixture into four ⅔-cup ramekins. Cover each ramekin with a small square of plastic wrap.

3 Bring a saucepan of water to a boil and place a steamer over the top, making sure the water doesn't touch it. Turn the heat down to low and steam the ramekins 10 to 12 minutes until the tops are just set. If bubbles start to appear, turn the heat down. Once cooked, remove the plastic wrap and serve immediately.

SERVES 4

1 cup plus 2 tablespoons milk
2 tablespoons granulated sugar
2 eggs, beaten
1-inch piece gingerroot, peeled

GOES WELL WITH

Roast Lebanese Leg of Lamb with
    Spiced Lentil Puree (page 97)
Guyi Cumin, Chili and Soy Ribs
    (page 112)
Sea Bass Ceviche (page 125)

Mango, Orange and Nutmeg Cheesecake

Cheesecake is luscious to eat but can be tricky to make. This is a very simple version that involves a bit of mixing and then lots of eating. The main flavors are fresh mango and orange, which are complemented by lots of freshly grated nutmeg. The nutmeg really brings out the sweetness of the mango. As a spice it works amazingly with anything creamy, so it's a real winner in a cheesecake.

1 Grease the bottom and side of an 8-inch round nonstick springform cake pan that is at least 4 inches deep and line the bottom with baking parchment. Put the graham crackers into a food processor and blend to a fine crumb. Tip the crumbs into a saucepan and rinse the food processor bowl.

2 Add the butter and granulated sugar to the crumbs, then place the pan over medium heat and mix together until the butter and sugar completely melt. Tip the mixture into the prepared cake pan, then push it down, using the back of a spoon, to form an even layer over the base. Refrigerate 30 minutes.

3 Meanwhile, put the mango and orange juice into the food processor bowl and blend to a puree. Pass the puree through a strainer and divide the mixture in two portions. Cover one portion and refrigerate to serve with the cheesecake when it's ready and return the other portion to the food processor bowl.

4 Put the cream cheese, confectioners' sugar and nutmeg into the food processor bowl with the puree and blend until smooth.

5 Scrape the cheese and mango mixture over the crust in the cake pan and refrigerate 8 hours, or overnight. When you are ready to serve, pop open the springform mechanism on the cake pan, carefully remove the side and slowly slip the cake off the base onto a serving plate. Sprinkle with finely grated fresh nutmeg, drizzle the remaining mango and orange puree over and serve.

SERVES 8 TO 10
7 tablespoons unsalted butter, plus extra for greasing
2½ cups crushed graham crackers
1 tablespoon granulated sugar
1 large mango, peeled, seeded and cut into chunks
3 tablespoons orange juice
2 pounds cream cheese
1 cup unsifted confectioners' sugar
¼ fresh nutmeg, finely grated, plus extra for sprinkling

GOES WELL WITH
Char-Grilled Cilantro and Mint Chicken (page 64)
Za'atar Lamb Cutlets (page 104)
Steamed Cod in a Banana Leaf (page 126)

Vanilla and Honey Syllabub

Syllabubs are actually very old British desserts that date all the way back to the Tudors in the fifteenth century. Traditionally, they were a mix of cream and wine, thought to be showstoppers when served at banquets. I have modernized my version with vanilla, and have used a little yogurt to keep it really light. The sweet honey and refreshing lemon get the mouth watering, while the vivid green pistachios provide just the right amount of color and crunch—definitely still a dessert to be noticed!

SERVES 4

1¼ cups heavy ream
3 tablespoons honey, plus extra to serve (optional)
juice of 2 lemons
zest of 1 lemon
7 tablespoons plain yogurt
1 vanilla bean
½ cup unsalted pistachio nuts, shelled and roughly chopped

GOES WELL WITH:

Vietnamese Chicken with Chili and Lemongrass (page 56)
Marinated Lamb Chops with a Spicy Mango Salsa (page 102)
Broiled Red Snapper with Mexican Salsa Verde and Corn Salad (page 131)

1 Pour the cream into a large mixing bowl and beat into firm peaks using a hand-held electric mixer.

2 In a separate small bowl, beat the honey and lemon juice together until well combined, then add the lemon zest and yogurt and mix well.

3 Using a sharp knife, split the vanilla bean in half, scrape the seeds into the yogurt mixture and mix until well combined.

4 Fold the yogurt into the cream, using a lage metal spoon, then divide the mixture into four glasses or bowls and refrigerate at least 30 minutes. Serve drizzled with honey, if liked, and pistachios sprinkled over the top.

Cardamom and Pistachio Nut Kulfi

1 Pour the evaporated milk into a saucepan and bring to a boil over medium heat. Tip in the cornstarch and sugar, reduce the heat to low and beat continuously until smooth. Continue to heat, stirring occasionally, 5 minutes longer, or until the mixture is slightly thickened.

2 Meanwhile, split the cardamom pods by pressing down on them with the back of a knife. Scrape out the seeds, crush them with the back of the knife and then finely chop them. Add the seeds to the evaporated milk mixture, along with the pistachio nuts and cream and mix well.

3 Transfer the mixture to a small plastic container with a lid. Cover and freeze 6 hours, or overnight. Remove from the freezer about 20 minutes before serving so the kulfi has a chance to soften. Alternatively, set the kulfi in four molds lined with plastic wrap.

SERVES 4

1¾ cups evaporated milk
1 tablespoon cornstarch
¼ cup sugar
3 cardamom pods
scant ¼ cup unsalted pistachio nuts, sliced, plus extra to serve
scant ½ cup heavy cream

GOES WELL WITH

Ciya Shish Kebab (page 94)
Chili and Basil Scallops (page 146)
Chana Masala (Indian Chickpeas) (page 164)

Mexican Cinnamon Peaches

SERVES 4
heaped ¾ cup sugar
3-inch piece cinnamon stick
4 ripe peaches
juice of 1 lemon
vanilla ice cream, to serve (optional)
    (see page 212)

GOES WELL WITH
Thai Red Duck Curry (page 81)
Fried Steaks with Black Pepper Dip
    (page 88)
Broiled Lamb Skewers with a Bulgur
    Wheat Salad (page 106)

1 Put the sugar and cinnamon into a large saucepan with 2 cups water and bring to a boil over medium heat until all the sugar dissolves. Reduce the heat to low and simmer 10 minutes.

2 Carefully add the peaches, cover and cook, turning occasionally, 5 minutes, or until they start to soften. Remove the peaches from the pan and set aside about 10 minutes. Once cool enough to handle, peel off the skins and put the skins back into the syrup, along with the lemon juice. The peach skins will give the syrup a lovely pink color. Simmer 5 minutes, then remove the cinnamon and simmer 13 to 15 minutes until the syrup is reduced right down and is really sticky.

3 Cut the peaches in half and gently tear the flesh away from the pits with your hands so it breaks into rough pieces. This gives you a great rustic look, rather than doing it neatly with a knife. Pour the fragrant syrup over and serve immediately with vanilla ice cream, if liked.

Cinnamon

This is an wonderful spice. It smells like Christmas and lends itself perfectly to both sweet and savory dishes, so it should come as no surprise that cinnamon has been in demand for thousands of years. The ancient Egyptians used the spice, which, at the time, was more expensive than gold, as an embalming agent, scent, cooking ingredient and medicine. It was prized throughout antiquity, and the cinnamon trade was strictly controlled by Arab traders. The ancient Greek historian Herodotus noted that cinnamon came from Arabia, where it was collected by giant birds from a strange island where the cinnamon trees grew, to build their nests. To get the cinnamon down from the trees, the Arab traders would offer cattle to the birds for them to eat. The huge birds would then sweep down, collect the cattle and return to their nests. The extra weight caused the cinnamon to fall down, so the brave traders could collect the precious quills.

Well, as far as I know, there are no giant birds involved in the production of cinnamon. In fact, cinnamon is the inner bark of a Sri Lankan tree. The outer bark is removed and the exposed inner bark is scraped off and dried. The best cinnamon, prized for its sweet taste and fine quills, is still from its native Sri Lanka.

Cinnamon is available in both sticks and ground. It's quite hard to grind yourself, so I recommend you always have both on hand. Cinnamon is something everyone seems to have, which is great. If, however, you find any cinnamon, or any spice for that matter, more than a year old lurking in the cupboard, please chuck it out and get some new, so you can do justice to the taste of such an amazing ingredient. If you keep cinnamon in a dry, airtight container out of direct sunlight, ground cinnamon will last about six months and the sticks about a year.

Tropical Fruit Salad with a Chili, Star Anise, Cinnamon and Lime Dressing

SERVES 4
scant ½ cup sugar
2-inch piece cinnamon stick
2 star anise
¼ chili flakes
juice of 2 limes
seeds and pulp of 3 passionfruit
1 mango, peeled, pitted and roughly
    chopped
½ pineapple, peeled, cored and roughly
    chopped
1 papaya, peeled, seeded and roughly
    chopped
plain yogurt, to serve

GOES WELL WITH
Chorizo and Squid Salad (page 45)
Broiled Monkfish Salad with a Red
    Pepper, Garlic and Chili Dressing
    (page 50)
Chicken in Macadamia Nut and
    Mustard Seed Sauce (page 73)

1 Put the sugar, cinnamon, star anise and chili flakes into a large pan with 1 cup water and bring to a boil over high heat. Stir continuously 1 minute, or until all the sugar dissolves, then reduce the heat to medium and simmer, shaking the pan occasionally, 10 minutes until the liquid reduces to a thin syrup. Transfer the syrup to a mixing bowl and set aside to cool. Remove the cinnamon to stop its flavor overpowering the dressing, but reserve for decoration, if liked.

2 Once the syrup is cool, pour in the lime juice and passionfruit and mix well. Add the mango, pineapple and papaya, then toss together so the spicy, sweet-sour flavors of the dressing coat the fruit.

3 Serve at room temperature or chilled with a generous dollop of yogurt and the star anise and cinnamon, if liked, arranged on top.

Cambodian Caramelized Ginger Bananas with Vanilla Ice Cream

SERVES 4
¾ cup sugar
4 bananas, peeled and halved
    lengthwise
1-inch piece gingerroot, peeled and
    thinly sliced

FOR THE VANILLA ICE CREAM
1 vanilla bean
1¼ cups light cream
4 egg yolks
½ cup sugar
1¼ cups heavy cream

GOES WELL WITH
Vietnamese Shrimp, Cucumber and
    Mint Salad (page 47)
Pueblan Almond Duck (page 82)
Fried Steaks with Black Pepper Dip
    (page 92)

1 To make the caramelized bananas, put the sugar and 6 tablespoons water into a shallow saucepan over medium heat. Melt the sugar, shaking the pan occasionally, until it is bubbling and syrupy and turns a caramel color.

2 Add the bananas, shake the pan and cook 1 minute. Remove the pan from the heat, scatter the ginger over and carefully spoon the sauce over the bananas in the pan. Leave 2 to 3 minutes so the sauce gets really sticky and the flavors develop.

3 Divide the bananas onto four serving plates and serve immediately with a few scoops of vanilla ice cream and any remaining caramelized sauce poured over. If the sauce starts to harden, then warm it over low heat 2 minutes until it goes goey again.

VANILLA ICE CREAM

1 To make the ice cream, scrape the seeds from the vanilla bean and add both the seeds and the pod to a saucepan along with the light cream. Mix well and bring to a boil over medium heat. Remove the pan from the heat and set to one side 15 minutes to allow the wonderful flavor of the vanilla to infuse with the cream.

2 Meanwhile, put the egg yolks and sugar into a large mixing bowl and beat until they turn pale and fluffy. Set aside.

3 Pour the heavy cream into a mixing bowl, beat into soft peaks and set aside.

4 Tip the egg yolks and sugar mix into the vanilla-infused cream and mix everything together really well. Reheat the cream mixture over low heat, stirring continuously, 6 to 8 minutes until it is thick enough to coat the back of the spoon. Carefully remove the vanilla bean and gently fold in the whipped heavy cream.

5 Transfer the mixture into a plastic container with a lid and set aside to cool completely. Cover and freeze 1 hour, then, using a fork, beat the ice cream to keep it really light. Repeat this again after another 2 hours, then return the ice cream to the freezer to set. Remove the ice cream from the freezer 10 minutes before serving.

Mayan Hot Chocolate

Chocolate is actually a very old ingredient. It is made from cocoa beans, which are the seeds of the Central American cacao tree. More than 2,000 years ago, the ancient Mayans would mix cocoa beans, chili and corn with water to make a potent drink. When the Spanish invaded the Americas in the sixteenth century, they took the chocolate drink back home and adapted it, replacing the Mayans' beloved chili with sugar, vanilla and cinnamon. By the seventeenth century, chocolate was considered a luxury item and the drink became all the rage across Europe—the wealthy would visit upscale "chocolate houses" to quaff the exotic drink in style.

Being a bit of a purist and a chili freak, I have combined the traditional sweet flavors of hot chocolate with the original chili for my recipe. Chili and chocolate work so well together and the addition of cinnamon and honey makes this a truly indulgent drink. It's a really full-on chocolate experience so you only need a small amount per person.

1 Put the milk, cream, cinnamon and chili flakes into a saucepan over low heat. Leave 15 to 20 minutesuntil the mixture is brought to a simmer—you only want a few tiny bubbles around the edge of the saucepan.

2 Meanwhile, break the chocolate into pieces and melt in a heatproof bowl set over a saucepan of barely simmering water. Make sure the bottom of the bowl doesn't touch the water.

3 Pour the melted chocolate into the hot milk mixture and add the honey. Gently stir until the drink is glossy and smooth and piping hot. Serve immediately.

SERVES 4
1 cup milk
1 cup light cream
¼ teaspoon ground cinnamon
a pinch of chili flakes
3 ounces chocolate with 70 to 80% cocoa
3 tablespoons honey

GOES WELL WITH
Pueblan Almond Duck (page 82)
Persian Saffron and Honey Lamb Stew (page 101)

Chili Passionfruit Martini

This is my favorite martini. I love the sweet-sour taste of the passionfruit against the background heat of the chili. I warn you, though, this is a very addictive drink, so it's worth making plenty of sugar syrup in advance!

SERVES 4
2½ cups sugar
8 passionfruit
scant 1 cup chilled vodka
1 red chili, seeded and roughly sliced,
   plus extra to serve

GOES WELL WITH
Tamarind and Lemongrass Chicken
   Stir-Fry (page 59)
Stir-Fried Beef with Black Pepper and
   Basil (page 89)
Creamy Cilantro Swordfish with a Red
   Onion Raita (page 123)

1 To make the sugar syrup, put the sugar in a small saucepan with 1 cup water. Bring to a slow boil over medium heat until the sugar dissolves, then set aside to cool.

2 Scoop the seeds and pulp from 6 of the passionfruit into a strainer over a small bowl. Stir and press down on the passionfruit with a spoon until all the juice is collected underneath.

3 Pour the passionfruit juice into a cocktail shaker, then add the vodka, red chili, sugar syrup and a handful of ice cubes. Shake well and then divide between four chilled martini glasses. Wash and halve the remaining 2 passionfruit and carefully position half a passion fruit in each glass, add a few strips of chili and serve.

Margarita on the Rocks with a Chili Rim

1 Put the tequila, Cointreau, lime juice and sugar in a cocktail shaker with lots of ice cubes and shake well.

2 Put the salt and chili powder into a spice grinder, grind to a fine powder and tip out onto a plate. Wet the rims of four margarita glasses with a slice of lime, then dip the glasses into the chili salt.

3 Drop a handful of ice into each martini glass, then strain the liquid over the top. Add a twisted strip of lime peel to each glass and serve immediately.

SERVES 4

1 cup plus 2 tablespoons tequila
$^2/_3$ cup Cointreau or other orange liqueur
juice of 2 limes, plus an extra slice
4 sugar
strips of lime peel, to serve

FOR THE CHILI RIM

2 tablespoons sea salt
2 chili powder

GOES WELL WITH

Vietnamese Shrimp, Cucumber and
    Mint Salad (page 47)
Al Pastor Pork and Pineapple Salad
    (page 110)
Szechuan Noodles with Lamb and
    Peanuts (page 190)

Lemongrass and Ginger Rum Cocktail

SERVES 4
4 lemongrass stalks
1¼ cups sugar
½-inch piece gingerroot, peeled
7 tablespoons light rum
juice of 2 limes
tonic water, for topping up

GOES WELL WITH
Pomegranate, Fennel, Orange and
    Watercress Salad (page 22)
Char-Grilled Cilantro and Mint
    Chicken (page 64)
Marinated Lamb Chops with a Spicy
    Mango Salsa (page 102)

1 Cut off the end of the lemongrass stalks and bash the fatter end of the lemongrass a couple of times with a heavy spoon to help release their delicious flavor. Put the lemongrass in a saucepan with the sugar and ¾ cup water and bring to a boil. Turn the heat down to low and simmer, shaking the pan occasionally, 4 to 5 minutes until all the sugar dissolves. Remove the pan from the heat and set aside to cool. You will end up with more sugar syrup than you need for four drinks, but it's important to cover the lemongrass stalks with enough water so you get the maximum flavor from them. The extra syrup will keep for a few days in the refrigerator.

2 Grate the ginger into a cocktail shaker, discarding any fibrous bits. Pour in the rum, juice from 1 of the limes and scant ¼ cup of the cooled lemongrass sugar syrup, then add the lemongrass stalks from the syrup and a handful of ice. Shake vigorously until the ingredients are well combined.

3 Divide the cocktail into four ice-filled rocks glasses, top up each glass with tonic water and serve with a lemongrass stalk from the shaker to act as a stirrer.

4 Squeeze the juice from the remaining lime into the four glasses and stir in with the lemongrass stalks. Serve immediately.

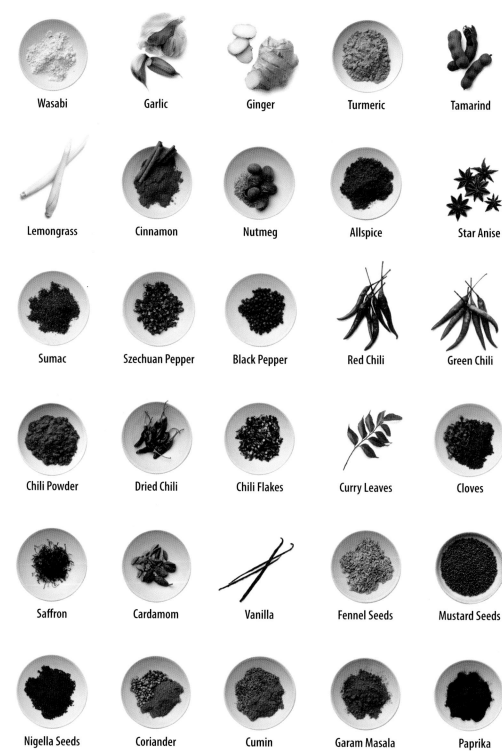

Wasabi Garlic Ginger Turmeric Tamarind

Lemongrass Cinnamon Nutmeg Allspice Star Anise

Sumac Szechuan Pepper Black Pepper Red Chili Green Chili

Chili Powder Dried Chili Chili Flakes Curry Leaves Cloves

Saffron Cardamom Vanilla Fennel Seeds Mustard Seeds

Nigella Seeds Coriander Cumin Garam Masala Paprika

Spice Directory

Wasabi The grated root of wasabi, the Japanese member of the horseradish family, is light green in color and has a strong, peppery flavor. Wasabi comes powdered or in a paste. I prefer to use the paste, as it's quicker to use and lasts well in the refrigerator. When you think of wasabi you probably think of sushi; however, it's also wonderful in dressings with soy sauce or lime juice, and is delicious mixed into mayonnaise. Be careful to avoid lumps of wasabi, though, or you'll get the dreaded "wasabi nose rush."

Garlic (see page 154) With its sharp, peppery, pungent taste, garlic is one of the most versatile spices and is an essential ingredient in most spice dishes. Fresh is definite best, especially if used raw.

Ginger (see page 140) Delicious in savory and sweet dishes, this bulbous root has a brilliant fresh, slightly peppery, fragrant taste and a sweet juicy smell.

Turmeric (see page 120) A root spice and part of the ginger family, turmeric adds an intense, deep orangy yellow to all dishes it is used in and a distinct earthy and slightly bitter flavor.

Tamarind Commonly thought of as a Southeast Asian souring agent, tamarind is actually used all over the world from India to Africa and Mexico to the Middle East. It comes from the fruit of a large brown, pealike pod that is soaked in water. The pulp is squeezed and strained, and it is the sour water that is used. You can buy good-quality tamarind pastes that you soak in warm water and strain before using. I'd avoid using tamarind concentrates, which are strong and very bitter. Once opened, keep the tamarind paste in the refrigerator. Use it within two months, or as directed on the package.

Lemongrass (see page 48) Available fresh, dried and powdered, the delicious, fragrant, lemony flavor of lemongrass comes from the pale-colored stalk. For maximum clear, lemony aroma and flavor the fresh version is best.

Cinnamon (see page 208) This fragrant spice has a sweet taste that works superbly in both savory and sweet dishes. It is available in quills (sticks) or ground.

Nutmeg Nutmeg is the seed of a small green fruit, which when broken open, reveals a shiny brown, buckeyelike shell, surrounded by a bright red mesh. The red mesh, once dried, is the spice mace and inside the shell is the nutmeg. Nutmeg is best bought whole and simply grated as and when required. You can buy small nutmeg graters with a built-in storage compartment, which will keep the nutmeg for more than a year. Nutmeg has a strong fragrance and slightly sweet, spice-heavy flavor that can be used in so many different ways. In Malaysia, nutmeg is used to make a pungent iced drink, it flavors briyanis and pilafs everywhere and works well with traditional white and cheese sauces. It's also delicious in desserts.

Allspice Allspice was originally named because its flavor was thought to be similar to the combination of several spices, including cinnamon, cloves and nutmeg. Allspice is actually a small, dried, unripened fruit, native to central America, and looks a bit like a large, reddish-brown peppercorn. It has a fantastic, aromatic, mixed spice flavor that is a key ingredient in Caribbean and Middle Eastern cooking. Readily available whole or ground, the whole spice will last about one year in a dry, airtight container when kept out of direct sunlight; the ground around six months.

Star Anise (see page 62) A beautiful looking and tasting spice, star anise is most used in fushion cooking to add an intense aniseed flavor and fresh note.

Sumac A dried, ground fruit, sumac is used in cooking all over the Middle East. It has a dark red color and a sour flavor, and is perfect to add to stews, which is what the Arab nomads used it for, instead of fresh juicy lemons. They also mixed it into yogurt and sprinkled it over meat and salads, to add a lively fresh taste. It is one of the major ingredients in the Arabic za'atar spice blend used to flavor everything from kebabs to breakfast bread. Sumac is bought ground and will last about six months in a dry, airtight container when kept out of direct sunlight.

Szechuan Pepper This awesome spice is the absolute star of Chinese cooking for me, providing an wonderful background heat that gives way to a highly addictive warm, mouth-numbing sensation. Adding a pinch of peppercorns into hot oil will provide you with all the flavor you need for stir-frys and sticky braised meat dishes. The whole spice will last about one year if kept in a dry, airtight container kept out of direct sunlight.

Black Pepper (see page 90) With its spicy pungency, black pepper can add a wonderful kick or gentle warm hint to almost any savory dish and some sweet dishes, too.

Chili (see page 24) Synonymous with spicy foods, the variety of red and green chilies available provide the choice of adding a warming, mild spicy hint to dishes or a full-on, hot chili punch.

Curry Leaves These green leaves have the flavor of Southern India locked inside them, ready to burst out when used either fresh or dried, and add a nutty aroma and savory flavor to a curry. The fresh leaves have the best taste, but can be difficult to find. Thankfully, they last in the freezer for a few months; simply add frozen to hot oil like other whole spices. The dried leaves have a milder flavor, so you need to use more of them. They will last up to six months in a dry, airtight container. To get the most out of curry leaves, rub them between your hands to break them up as you add them to a curry.

Cloves (see page 184) This spice adds sweet, woody, rich flavor and aroma to savory and sweet dishes, but because the flavor is big cloves shouldn't be used too liberally.

Saffron This spice is the bright orange stigma of the purple-colored saffron crocus. It has a pungent, grassy flavor and adds a rich deep-orange color to stews, curries and rice dishes. It takes between 70,000 and 80,000 of the flowers to produce 1 pound saffron, which has to be handpicked to avoid damage, making it the most expesive of all the spices. Saffron is very strong and can overpower a dish, so a little goes a long way. When kept in a cool, dry, dark place, your saffron will last more than a year.

Cardamom The lovely green cardamom pods have a distinctive sweet flavor that is perfect in both sweet and savory dishes. It is used whole, ground or, in some cases, just for the seeds inside. When cooking with whole cardamoms, to release all the flavor of the little seeds in the pod, press down on the pods, using the side of a knife onto a cutting board, so they split open, revealing the tasty seeds. If you only need the seeds, scrape them out at this point and discard the husk. Cardamom is a key ingredient in many spice blends, but it can be hard to grind into a powder—simply remove any little pieces of husk that don't break up. When kept in a cool, dry, dark place, cardamom pods will last about six months, but as soon as they begin to lose their green color they also loose their flavor.

Vanilla This spice, from the orchid family, is a long, thin fruit that eveals hundreds of tiny back seeds when split open. The seeds can be scraped out and added to a plethora of things to give them an aroma and flavor unlike anything else. You can also buy vanilla extract, and a really good-quality one works well; the essence, however, is not worth getting involved with. Vanilla beans last up to six months in a dry, airtight container if kept in the dark.

Fennel Seeds These are little green-colored seeds that have a most amazing, fresh aniseed flavor. Fennel seeds are used as a major component in Chinese five spice and in mukhwas in India, a mix of nuts and seeds that is served after a meal to help freshen breath and aid digestion. Their flavor works incredibly well with pork and fish, and the seeds can be added whole or ground to really lift their flavors. In a cool, dry, dark place, the seeds will last about one year. The ground spice will last less than six months.

Mustard Seeds There are three types of mustard seed: black, brown and white. The brown and white are actually both yellow in color and are what we know from jars of mustard. You can also buy beautifully golden yellow mustard oil, which is often used in North Indian cuisine. I have only used the black mustard seeds for my book. When added to hot oil, they crackle gently and give a nutty, slightly peppery taste that's a great background flavor. When kept in a dry, airtight container away from direct sunlight, mustard seeds will last more than a year.

Nigella Seeds These black seeds are sometimes called black cumin or onion seeds. They have a slightly bitter, oregano herblike taste and provide a brilliant crunchy texture. Nigella seeds are used extensively in Indian and Middle Eastern cooking, adding flavor to curries, legumes, stews, breads, salads, pickles and chutneys. The seeds are bought whole and can be used without dry roasting, although this will enhance the flavor. They will last about year in a dry, airtight container kept out of direct sunlight.

Coriander The mild, slightly orangey, fragrant flavor of coriander comes from the coriander seed and is completely different from the herb cilantro, which is also called "coriander" in some countries. The spice can be used whole, crushed or ground, and is best friends with cumin as far as Indian cooking is concerned. In Europe, this spice is used to flavor gin, in Thailand it is added to green curry pastes, in Ethiopia the seeds are ground up and added to the Ethiopian spice mix berbere and it is an essential part of Arabic baharat spice blends. The whole spice will last about one year in a dry, airtight container kept out of direct sunlight; the ground spice less than six months.

Cumin (see page 76) The cumin seed is used whole and ground, and the earthy, nutty flavor and pungent aroma of this spice make it an essential ingredient in most curry powders.

Garam Masala A classic Indian blend of strong spices, garam masala includes cloves, cardamom, cinnamon, nutmeg and black pepper. It's used to give body and depth of flavor to a curry, and is often added at the end of the cooking process to liven things up. There is no standard recipe; it varies from region to region and household to household—everyone has their own version that is always the right one! Thankfully, we can buy good-quality, preground garam masala easily. It adds a wonderful hit of spice-heavy seasoning without the need for keeping hundreds of spices on hand. The ground version is also easy to find, but it won't be quite as fragrant as the preground. When kept in a cool, dry, dark place, garam masala will last up to six months.

Paprika Made from ground, dry red capsicum peppers, paprika provides a deep-red color and comes in several different flavors: hot, mild, sweet and smoked. Like all capsicum species, it arrived in Spain from the Americas and its use spread to color and flavor soups, stews and rice all over the world. The spice works really well in rubs: think Indian tandoori chicken. I really love it mixed with thyme, garlic, lemon juice and olive oil and smothered on any meat, fish or vegetables. Smoked paprika has a much stronger flavor, like a barbecue in a box, and should be used sparingly. The vibrant red color is a wonderful garnish for salads and dips. Paprika will retain its flavor up to six months if kept in a dry, airtight container, out of direct sunlight.

Index

Acknowledgments

Family and friends for putting up with me
The Hung's in China
All the guys at Shinta Mani Hotel in Cambodia
Suman in Jaipur
Chef Nooror in Bangkok
Nazlina in Malaysia
All the Talwar family in NY and Delhi
Nitya
Nimmy and Paul and their amazing Syrian Christian family
Sarath and Nalini Alwis for sorting everything out in Sri Lanka
Souk Talwa in Beirut
Jon and Estella in Mexico
Grace at Duncan Baird
Everyone at Limelight